D0413208

Official Publisher Partnership

OCR
Computing FOR A LEVEL

Chris Leadbetter
Agneau Belanyek
George Rouse

YORK COLLEGE

128806

YORK COLLEGE

STAMPED CAT.

ACC. No. 128806

CLASS No. 004 LEA

LEARNING RESOURCE
CENTRE

The Publishers would like to thank the following for permission to reproduce copyright material:

Photo credits: p.34 *t* © David R. Frazier Photolibrary, Inc./Alamy; **p.34** *b*, **37**, **38**, **55** *t* Steve Connolly; **p.39** © Helene Rogers/Alamy; **p.55** *b* © Bettmann/Corbis; **p.56** Arthur Tsang/AFP/Getty Images; **p.57** Software Production Associates Ltd.; **p.63** © totalphoto/Alamy; **p.69** © Helen King/Corbis; **p.75** Nintendo; **p.128** Naval Historical Center; **p.188** Chabruken/Taxi/Getty Images; **p.191** *t* Microsoft/Visual Basic, **c** Sun Microsystems/Java, *b* Ruby; **p.193** *t* Leland Bobbe/The Image Bank/Getty Images; **p.195** Frederic Cirou/Photoalto/ Photolibrary Group; **p.196** © Tim Pannell/Corbis; **p.198** BLOOMimage/Getty Images; **p.199** Imagesource/Photolibrary Group; **p.202** © moodboard/Corbis; **p.206** Purestock/Photolibrary Group.

Questions from past examination papers reproduced with kind permission of OCR.

Every effort has been made to trace all copyright holders, but if any have been inadvertently overlooked the Publishers will be pleased to make the necessary arrangements at the first opportunity.

t = top, *b* = bottom, *l* = left, *r* = right

Although every effort has been made to ensure that website addresses are correct at time of going to press, Hodder Education cannot be held responsible for the content of any website mentioned in this book. It is sometimes possible to find a relocated web page by typing in the address of the home page for a website in the URL window of your browser.

Hatchette's policy is to use papers that are natural, renewable and recyclable products and made from wood grown in sustainable forests. The logging and manufacturing processes are expected to conform to the environmental regulations of the country of origin.

Orders: please contact Bookpoint Ltd, 130 Milton Park, Abingdon, Oxon OX14 4SB. Telephone: (44) 01235 827720. Fax: (44) 01235 400454. Lines are open 9.00 – 5.00, Monday to Saturday, with a 24-hour message answering service. Visit our website at www.hoddereducation.co.uk

© Christopher Leadbetter, Agneau Belanyek and George Rouse 2008

First published in 2008 by
Hodder Murray, an imprint of Hodder Education,
a member of the Hodder Headline Group
338 Euston Road
London NW1 3BH

Impression number   5 4 3 2

Year   2012 2011 2010 2009

All rights reserved. Apart from any use permitted under UK copyright law, no part of this publication may be reproduced or transmitted in any form or by any means, electronic or mechanical, including photocopying and recording, or held within any information storage and retrieval system, without permission in writing from the publisher or under licence from the Copyright Licensing Agency Limited. Further details of such licences (for reprographic reproduction) may be obtained from the Copyright Licensing Agency Limited, Saffron House, 6-10 Kirby Street, London EC1N 8TS.

Cover photo ©Andrey Prokhorov/istockphoto.com

Typeset in Stone Sans 11pt by DC Graphic Design Ltd, Swanley Village, Kent

Printed in Italy

A catalogue record for this title is available from the British Library

ISBN-13: 978 0340 967 898

Contents

Unit 4 The Project

Chapter 1 Components of a Computer System

All computer systems need two types of component if they are to do anything useful. There are the physical parts that can be touched and seen, like the computer tower or the printer. These are called the computer **hardware** for no better reason than they are hard. Then there are the instructions that the hardware needs to tell it what to do, which are collected together in groups of instructions called **programs**, and they are all known as the **software** of the system.

The basis of Chapter 1 is that we should understand the difference between these types of component and that we should learn a little about each one. The emphasis is on the 'little'; more detailed information will be given in Chapters 2 and 4, which are entitled 'Software' and 'Hardware'.

It is also important to learn some of the specialist vocabulary that is used to split the software and the hardware into smaller divisions.

The items of hardware in a computer system can be divided into one of four groups:

- The computer itself
- The peripherals, which simply means that these are *outside* the computer. There are three sorts of peripheral:
  - input devices, so that the computer can be told what to do and the data to be used
  - output devices, so that the computer can tell us what it has done or it can control some device to do something useful, like alter the central heating because it is too hot
  - storage devices, so that the computer can remember what it is meant to do when it is switched back on after having been turned off, otherwise by the time you tried to give it a second instruction it would have forgotten the first.

The software comes in two main types:

- The operating system or system software. These are the programs that allow the hardware to work.
- The applications software, which is the set of programs that allow the user to do something useful with the computer.

1　a State what is meant by:

　　(i)　hardware

　　(ii)　software

　　in a computer system.　(2)

　b Explain why a storage device is needed on most computer systems.　(2)

OCR AS Computing paper 2506 – June 2006

2　a State what is meant by:

　　(i)　systems software　(1)

　　(ii)　applications software.　(1)

　b Give an example of a type of applications software and state what it might be used for.　(2)

OCR AS Computing paper 2506 – June 2006

Chapter 2 Software

1. The systems development life cycle

When a new system is being produced it is important to ensure that some sort of plan is kept to. This is true no matter how complicated the system is. If you are putting up a shelf it is important that the holes are drilled in the wall, then the wallplugs are put in the holes and then the brackets are screwed into the plugs. Finally the shelf is put on the brackets. This is a small job, probably done many times before by the person putting the shelf up and it only needs one person to do it. A manual of how to do it and in what order to do the different steps is not needed, in fact if there was one that came with the shelf most people would throw it away before they start.

Creating a set of instructions for telling someone else how to do something that you find natural to do is a very complex skill.

The example of putting up a shelf is a task you would almost do without thinking. The task of actually thinking about doing it makes the task hard. Another example is asking a driver to start the car moving while they tell you in detail what they are doing; it is almost impossible.

Creating a new computer system is rather more complicated than putting up a shelf or typing a letter, so it is a good idea to have a set of rules to follow which will make sure that everything is done in the right order and that nothing is forgotten. One such set of rules is written as a series of stages that need to be followed in order to produce the desired system. It is called the **systems development life cycle**. There are two standard ways of describing the process and they are known as the **waterfall** and **spiral** models.

Often, when a task is being carried out it is being done for another person. If this is the case then it adds complexity to the task because two people now have to work together so there is more chance of a mistake. I know how to put up a shelf but if I am putting up one for my aged aunt then she has an input into the solution to the problem. She is the one who knows what sort of shelf she wants, she knows where it should go and at what height. I am the one who has the skill to realise that this is a partition wall and so needs a special type of plug, which will require a particular diameter of drill bit, and so on. My aunt is the one with knowledge about the problem whereas I am the one with knowledge about the solution. The same is true if the problem is made larger, as with the creation of a new computer solution for a business. The person with the problem knows what the problem is, after all they are the ones who have been living with the problem, but they may not have a lot of computer

< Discuss >

Without touching a computer, try to produce a set of instructions for typing a properly formatted letter into a piece of word processing software.

6

< Discuss >

Why is it called a 'cycle'? Try to explain this.

knowledge, so a specialist in solving problems with a computer is employed to oversee the solution. This specialist is called a systems analyst. In reality the systems analyst may be in charge of a team of people, all of whom have different skills, but for the purposes of this work we will assume that the analyst is working alone.

At each stage of the cycle try to relate the task needed to be done at that stage with the problem of putting up the shelf for an aged aunt. The analogy will be a bit difficult at times. This reflects what happens in real life when, for most problems, not all the stages are relevant, but it will be possible for most of the stages.

< Discuss >

Why is the language used in the problem definition so important?

a Problem definition: the analyst and the client must establish between them what the problem is that should be solved. The client knows what the problem is that they want solved while the analyst knows what is possible. This is the most important stage of all because if the problem is not sensibly defined then it may not be solvable or the solution may not do what the client wants. If the analyst and the client do not work together then either the solution will not work, or it may work and yet not solve the problem.

b Feasibility study: once the problem has been defined the analyst knows what they have to do. They must then decide whether or not it is going to be possible to solve the problem.

< Discuss >

Not all of these factors are relevant to the shelf problem, but there are probably more than you at first think.

- Is the technology available to solve it? (If it is not possible because a disk drive that large does not exist, then why bother trying?)
- Is it economically possible? (Will the solution be so expensive that it bankrupts the company? or: Will the added costs to production mean that the products produced are too expensive for people to buy?)
- What are the social effects? (If the solution will put a lot of people out of work then the governmental authorities may not allow it anyway.)
- Are there enough skilled people to run the system once it has been produced?
- What will be the effect on the customer? (If they are not going to see a difference, is there really any point in spending so much money? Basically, does a problem really exist?)

c Information collection: once the analyst and the client are both convinced that a solution is both possible and desirable, the analyst needs to collect information about the problem so that they not only understand the problem better but they also understand the present solution and what is wrong with it that requires some improvement. There are a number of ways in which the systems analyst finds out the information that they need to know.

< Discuss >

What are the sensible types of data collection for the shelf problem? Create a list of the advantages and disadvantages of each of the methods of information collection.

- **Interviews:** if there are a small number of important people to ask about the problems then interviews may be held. These take a long time and can be disconcerting for the people involved but it does allow the analyst to alter the direction of the questioning if something unplanned arises in the answers given and it also allows the interviewee to give information outside what the analyst was originally planning. Take particular note of the idea that an interview is like a conversation and should not be too carefully scripted because you are going to have to conduct one as part of the major project in Module 4.
- **Questionnaires:** (not 'surveys'). These allow the analyst to ask the opinions of a large number of people in a short time. It also means that those asked feel as though their views are being considered. However, they are very restrictive because the questions must be planned in advance.
- **Meetings:** a compromise between the mass participation of a questionnaire and the restrictive participation of interviews. Meetings allow a number of people to be able to voice their concerns without it being too time consuming. It is possible, however, that one or two participants who have particular views can control the meeting and make the results biased.
- **Observation:** the analyst watches the present practice, allowing them to form their own opinions. The difficulty is that this can be time consuming, people do not perform naturally when they are being watched and problems with the system may be cyclical in nature, so may be missed.
- **Documentation:** the analyst collects the available documentation and studies it. This will show how the system collects, processes and presents data and information.

< Topics for discussion >

The system flow chart for the shelf problem will look very different depending on the problem definition. Discuss how the flow chart will change according to the problem.

Produce a system flow chart for the problem.

Why is it not sensible to produce a data flow diagram?

d **Analysis:** once the information is collected, it must be analysed to decide what is important and what is not, or to put it another way, what is relevant to the problem that has been specified. The analyst will use diagrams to help in the understanding of the present system, both data flow diagrams (DFDs) and system flow charts. This analysis results in the analyst producing a **requirements specification**, which is a list of all the things which the solution is intended to produce. It is important to make sure that the client agrees with this requirements specification and with all the other decisions made at this stage, because these outcomes are going to be used to decide whether the solution satisfies the solution to the problem and whether or not the analyst gets paid.

e **Design:** notice that nothing has yet been said about how the problem is going to be solved. Everything has been about the problem and the present solution. Now we look at the ideas for the new solution. These ideas are known as the **design**

< Discuss >

The design section (e) does not seem to be relevant because I am the expert so why do I need this, why can't I just get on and do it?

specification. They lay down the content, the order and the relationships between the parts of the proposed solution. Once again, diagrams will be used here and they will look very like the diagrams in the analysis section (d). For example, a DFD will be drawn. The difference is that the DFD in the analysis section (d) described how the data used to flow whereas the DFD here will describe the data flow around the new solution. Included here will be the way that the data will be collected, input and stored (notice the use of the word 'data' rather than 'information'). The processing that will be carried out on it and the form in which it will be presented to the user needs to be designed.

f **Implementation:** the analyst will often turn the design over to a specialist whose job it is to produce a solution which is based on the design. This specialist may be expert on programming and methods of handling data, but, ultimately, will only be following the instructions given by the analyst. If the solution is going to be very complex it may be necessary to employ a team of people to produce the finished system. This will mean that there is an added difficulty in trying to coordinate the work done by different people. Imagine two programmers writing different parts of the software and they both use a variable name TOTAL, but standing for different things. This would be where bugs can develop as one version of TOTAL is changed and means that when TOTAL is used in the other part of the program it doesn't have the value that was expected. For reasons like this it is essential that the team maintain a set of written rules and actions taken so that they can ensure that problems are not going to arise. This is the first piece of written documentation that we are going to mention; there are two more to come.

< Discuss >

Why is the testing stage important to all involved?

g **Evaluation:** once the solution has been produced it must be evaluated to decide whether or not it adequately solves the problem that was set. This can be achieved by testing. There are many methods of testing and of deciding what should be tested, which will be covered in Chapter 3 of this unit and Chapter 12 of Unit 2. The important thing to realise is that the aim of testing, as far as the analyst is concerned, is to prove to the client that the solution works, not the quality of the solution or all the routes through it or any other reason. If the client accepts it then the analyst gets paid! This is sometimes called functional testing and if the client accepts that all the items in the requirements solution are met then the solution is said to be fully tested.

h **Installation:** the analyst must decide how to install the system into the business. This will include considerations of the purchase of hardware, the creation of the data files, the training of the staff, the method of changeover from the old system to the new and the consideration of future maintenance of the system.

i Maintenance: the system is now working and has been installed in the organisation for which it was designed. Sooner or later it will become obsolete which will mean the whole process will be started again, but while it is operated the system needs to be maintained.

Throughout the process the analyst must ensure that two further types of documentation, apart from that produced by the writing teams during the production of the software, are produced:

■ The technical documentation will be a set of documents that are designed for a person who is computer literate, probably the person who will be responsible for maintaining and improving the system once it is operating. The documentation will consist of things like lists of variable names that are being/have been used. This is essential if more than one programmer is working on the project because they will need to use the same variables. Also necessary in the finished documentation will be the program code, fully annotated to explain to the reader the purpose of each section/line of code. Data structures must be explained and justified. Testing procedures must be stated and the results given so that they can be repeated to ensure that the same results are obtained in the future.

Think in terms of a technician being called in because the checkouts at the local superstore have stopped accepting bar codes printed at the meat counter. The technician cannot solve the problem unless they know how the system is meant to work. Similarly, imagine that the store is undergoing an expansion and is to sell 50,000 different products instead of 30,000. This will have a major effect on the way that the system stores and searches the data. The technician will need to know how the structures work before being able to change them. Imagine also that the central office changes the operating system used on their computer systems – what will be the effect on the store computers and the communications between the store and central office? These are normal problems encountered in the use of computers by businesses, all of which require specialist personnel to solve them and also require those personnel to have specialist knowledge both about systems in general but also about the system in particular and that is where the need for a technical manual comes in.

■ The second type of documentation is the user documentation, which should accompany the system and give the user basic instructions about how to use the system. It will contain instructions relating to the users' view of the system rather than any indications about the underlying software. Contents will generally include how to wire up and look after the hardware, input and output formats and a list of error messages with

< Discuss >

What should the exact contents of the user guide for a typical system, for instance for the checkout till in a supermarket, include?

Why would your list of contents for a user guide not score very well in Question 3?

Note: This work on creating systems should be studied again when the project is being done in the second year of the course.

advice as to what to do, general maintenance tasks and where to get help if necessary. The user guide will be written in a language appropriate to the users' ability rather than in computer jargon.

END OF CHAPTER QUESTIONS

1 a State **two** stages of the systems life cycle, other than information collection. (2)
   b Describe **one** of the stages that you gave in part (a). (2)
   c Give an advantage and a disadvantage of using interviews to collect information. (2)
   d State **one** other method of information collection and give an advantage and a disadvantage of the method you have chosen. (3)
2 State **three** items that would be expected in a design specification and explain the purpose of each. (6)
3 Explain the purpose of user documentation. (4)

2. Generic applications software

< Discuss >

What types of generic software are available in school?

What uses are the generic software put to?

What, non-generic applications software is used in school departments and school administration? Why is generic software not available for these uses?

< Discuss >

What are the advantages and disadvantages of off-the-shelf and custom-written software in different circumstances?

Computer software is simply a set of instructions that allows the user to do something useful with a computer system. Some of this software is designed for a narrow set of applications, a good example of which would be a computer game. On the other hand some software is designed to be used for a wide variety of different application areas. This second type of applications software is known as **generic software** because it has a relatively large number of different uses. An example of a piece of generic software would be a word processor. This allows for document creation, letter writing, poster creation, creation of emails and many more uses. In other words the software has been created to allow the user to tailor the use to their specific needs as opposed to the software that we met in Chapter 2.1, where the whole point was to create software that would carry out a particular task.

Software can be further divided into two types: off-the-shelf and custom-written. Off-the-shelf is available for immediate use, like a word processor, while custom-written is specifically produced to solve a particular example of a problem. Custom-written software would be characterised by having to go through a full systems analysis process because it is a 'one-off'. An example application might be software to control a specific process on a production line. The process may well be the only one of its kind, so the software is unlikely to be for sale in the local computer shop, whereas everyone who uses a computer probably has a word processor, so you can go and buy one. Indeed, with a word processor it is a positive benefit having the same one as everyone else because then every computer can share documents. What good would it be if I could write beautiful emails, but nobody could read them?

Some software is designed to be able to store vast amounts of data about a particular topic and then to be able to interrogate it so that sensible information can be gleaned from that data. This type of software is called **knowledge-based software**. The data will be collected from experts in the field and the software will be used to replace the experts in conditions where the expert is unavailable. Typical uses would be to provide medical diagnoses or to interpret geological data to find specific requirements such as positions of possible oil resources.

3. Operating systems

A computer is simply a mass of metal, plastic and glass until it is supplied with the instructions telling it how to do something. This would be a piece of applications software like those mentioned in Chapter 2.2. However, a word processor may tell the computer that a letter 'A' is needed, but what is an 'A'? How does the screen work? Where are these instructions anyway? How does the computer read them? Where should the 'A' go? There needs to be something else, between the hardware and the applications programs that allows one to be run on the other. This 'thing' is called the **operating system** and it was mentioned in Chapter 1. The operating system (we shall call it the OS for simplicity) provides a platform on which the applications software can run. It controls the hardware and allows communication with the outside world.

A computer is a machine; a car is another type of machine. There is an OS in charge of the computer and there is a driver in charge of a car. Just as the same car will behave differently depending on the person driving it, the same computer will behave differently dependent on the type of OS that is used to run it.

Single-user/multi-tasking operating system

The computer that you probably have at home is likely to be running a **single user operating system**, so named because only one user can use it at a time, not because you are the only person who can ever use it! It will allow you (and any other users) to protect your files with things like passwords and will ensure that you are able to carry out actions with the hardware and use the software that you want to. In fact the single user OS on your computer is probably a bit more sophisticated than that. It will allow you to do more than one thing at a time like have a word processor on the screen and allow you to import a spreadsheet into it while playing some music to entertain you while you are working and also be logged onto the internet so that it can tell you when a message arrives. Basically it is doing more than one thing at a time and is called a **multi-tasking OS**.

We must always remember that computer processors can carry out so many processes in a given period of time that they are rarely used to their full potential. This work will be expanded upon in Chapter 15 but that is enough for this unit.

Batch processing

The first attempt at improving the efficiency of processing was to take away the slowest part of the process (the human being) and to use some other method to first collect all the input data. Once the data has been collected it could be input to the processor using the fastest input devices available. In this way one processor can be used to satisfy the demands of a number of users, although it may be some time before a response is produced as all the input data has to be collected before processing is done. A good example is when workers input the times at which they start work and finish work each day during the week. This data is collected in some way and then input into the computer and only when all the data has been collected is it used to calculate the pay for each worker for the week. This type of OS is obviously very different from the single user system although the computer itself may be exactly the same. The OS which insists on data being collected together first and then all input together is called a **batch OS**. Batch OSs were developed because in the 1950s there were very few computers but a lot of people wanting to use them. The only way to satisfy the demand was to stop people slowing the computer down.

Multi-user operating system

Nowadays there is another reason for wanting to let lots of people all use the same computer at the same time. If a database of information needs to be stored centrally and accessed by many people then one way is to use a **multi-user OS**. A good example of this would be a supermarket checkout system. All the checkouts need to have access to the same set of information: the stock file. The way it is done is that each of the terminals (the tills) are given a little bit of time on the computer before it goes on and gives the next till a bit of time. This can be repeated for however many tills there are before going back to the first one again. Remember that the computer processor is capable of very fast processing which allows it to do everything a till needs in about 1/100th of a second. This means that the human beings involved in the process do not notice and they think that the terminal at the till is concentrating on their shopping all the time.

Networking and distributed systems

Another way of sharing the same information is to network a number of computers so that they can all share the same resources. This is probably the same sort of system that you are taught on in school. When you switch your computer on and identify yourself the first thing that needs to happen is that software and data files need to be downloaded from a central resource onto your particular machine. After that your machine can work independently of the rest of the network because it is a computer, unlike the terminals in a multi-user system which all rely on one central computer for all their processing. We will be coming back to the subject of networking in Chapter 5 when we will also be discussing in more detail the idea of a distributed system which uses all the resources, both processing and storage, to distribute jobs around a system. This means that not only are resources like processing used efficiently but also that files needing storage are spread around a system to overcome the problem of having bottle necks when all the machines on the network are asking for information at the same time.

All the systems that we have looked at so far are designed to make use of the computer's amazing speed at processing to do more than one thing at a time. Sometimes there are applications where this is not sensible because the application being serviced needs immediate responses. An example would be a computer game where a driver has to drive a car around a motor racing circuit. Any decisions made by the driver must be acted on immediately otherwise the car will go off the road. A system like this is called a **real time OS** and is defined as an OS that produces an output immediately so that the output can influence the next input.

4. User interfaces

One of the jobs of the OS is to allow communication between the processor and the outside world. This may be as basic as connecting the processor to the various sensors and motors of a washing machine or it may be creating the information screen for communicating with a human being. It is this form of communication that we are interested in here and when the communication is with a human being the interface is called a **Human Computer Interface** or HCI. There are many different types of HCI and they are all designed to solve different problems for different types of users.

Graphical User Interface

The first type is a **Graphical User Interface** (GUI). GUIs are characterised by having little drawings, or graphics, called icons that appear on the screen. Each icon stands for different pieces of software or files that are available to the user. This type of HCI in which icons can be selected using a mouse, or some other pointer, makes identification and selection of applications very simple for the user. When the icon is selected there is a set of computer instructions accessed which the user cannot see.

< Activity >

An interesting exercise is to try to isolate one of the pieces of code behind an icon and see if you can work out precisely what it is doing. Also try to create a piece of code which you should hide behind an icon and which will change the screen resolution when the icon is selected.

The effect of these instructions is to run the application or file that has been selected and to show the output in an area of the screen which can be controlled by the user. This area of the screen is called a Window because the effect is like looking at a particular part of a large application through a window. Not all the options can be represented sensibly by icons because the screen is of limited size and if there are too many icons on the screen the user tends to forget what they all stand for. Some of the possible options, therefore, need to be offered to the user in some other way. One way is to have areas of the screen where, if they are pointed at with the cursor, a set of options, called a menu, will appear.

Put all these things together (Windows, Icons, Menus, Pointer) and you get another name for this type of interface, a 'WIMP'.

Most HCIs are GUI/WIMP these days. GUIs have the advantages of being easy to control because of the use of the pointer to select things and that they are universally understood.

Menu-based interface

Menu-based interfaces are often confused with GUIs for the obvious reason that GUIs have menus. The difference is that in a menu-based interface, the whole interface is designed as a set of menus. Imagine a tourist information screen at a train station. The first screen may offer information about sites to visit, places to stay, places to eat and transportation services. This is a menu. If the user selects places to stay the screen will change and offer hotels, guesthouses or bed and breakfast. If the user selects hotels the screen may change to offer different price ranges and so on until the details of a single hotel are shown. Menu-based interfaces are characterised by a set of different screens placed in layers for the user to negotiate through. Each screen will normally have a 'back' option to go back to the previous screen and a 'home' option to allow the user to go back to the start. Menu-based interfaces are very useful because they limit the users' choices and can be used by people who are computer illiterate. They also make it impossible for the user to find their way into places in the system that they should not be in. Because menu-based interfaces offer limited choices and a simple means of selection they are often used with a touch screen. Typically they are used in information systems, quiz games, simple computer systems offering few pieces of applications software, websites and many others where choices can be limited to a small number and the users may well be technologically unsophisticated.

Form-based interface

Imagine a website where you have just selected a DVD you want to purchase. You now have to arrange for payment by some method. The site will ask for information from you. You will be faced with a series of boxes where you have to type in the information needed. The boxes will be in an obvious order, either left to right or down the page, and each one will have some instructions about what to type in. The screen is laid out like a data capture form, the only difference is that the form is on the screen instead of on paper. This is called a **form-based interface**. The characteristics of a form-based interface are exactly as stated in our example. There will be a set of areas to fill in. They must be completed in a particular order and the interface is probably set up so that it will not allow you to go on to the next box until you have filled in the previous ones. In this way it can make sure that it gets all the information. If the boxes are split up properly then it also makes validation (Chapter 3.2) easier. It is difficult to automatically check that an address follows certain rules because there are so many ways of writing addresses. But if the address is split up so that each part is typed in separately it becomes much easier to check that the input is sensible. For instance the postcode can be checked that it is letter(s), number(s), letter(s), number(s) and anything else would be rejected.

Natural language interface

Some interfaces are quite complex for humans to use because they are designed so that the computer can understand them easily. If you think about a GUI it is only easy to use if you use it a lot and get used to it. The idea of having symbols that stand for different things and choosing them by double-clicking is not really natural for human beings. We would normally use a spoken language to communicate. An interface which allows humans to use our own language to communicate what we want to do and which relies on the computer to understand what it is talking about is called a **natural language interface**. It may be a spoken interface using speech recognition software for understanding spoken input and speech production software to create the output, or it may simply produce words on the screen and rely on the user typing in human language. This is very processor intensive and requires the computer to understand some of the syntax behind human language which is very difficult and can lead to misunderstandings. Because of its complexity it is only used when absolutely necessary. A good example would be to provide a spoken interface for blind people.

All the interfaces we have so far covered have two things in common:

1 They all restrict the user in some way. If you are using the school network system it is probable that the interface you are offered when the machine is switched on is a GUI. The main reason is not that it makes it simpler for you to use; it is rather, that it makes it impossible, or at least very difficult, for you to get into the OS and change things which should not be changed.

2 They all require processing power to a greater or lesser extent in order to turn the user requests into usable actions.

Command line interface

The final HCI we will consider is called the **command line interface**. The command line interface consists of a blank screen with a simple prompt which encourages the user to input a command to the OS. The commands are in text form and are specific to that OS. Think in terms of the user being the one who has to learn the commands this time instead of the OS. Using these commands the whole system is available to the user and the commands can be carried out quickly because specific commands can be used which do not involve going through a series of stages to get to the place in the system that the user requires. This sort of HCI would, typically, be used by a technician who is looking after a system and who will need to get everywhere in the system in order to carry out maintenance tasks.

With all interfaces that are to be used by human beings it is important to ensure that the fallibilities of the human are taken into account when they are designed. Human beings cannot handle a lot of information at the same time so filling a screen with too much information has the opposite to the desired effect – instead of giving the user more information it gives less because the user cannot decide which piece of information to look at. It is important that designers of interfaces follow certain rules when they are producing an interface. The information is normally presented with the most important in the top left-hand portion of the screen. This is because we naturally read from left to right and down the page so our eyes immediately go to the top of the page.

Red is a colour normally used to attract attention so it tends to be used for very important messages. Similarly, flashing text or text which is white on a black background will attract attention as long as it is sparingly used. When selecting images for the icons, what may be obvious to one person might not be to another and so care must be taken in selecting the images so as not to cause confusion.

< Discuss >

When may this not be a sensible screen arrangement?

< Discuss >

Bring up a word processor screen on a computer and the menu bar that allows drawing to be done. Discuss the different icons that are used. Which are obvious? Which did people have difficulty in interpreting? What is it about the design of the icons that is difficult? Try to redesign those that proved difficult.

The control room of a particular nuclear power station is full of screens and dials and graphical readouts and alarm systems. The most important part of the HCI is an old fashioned dot matrix printer which sits beside the controller's chair. It is only used for the most critical of messages. The hope is that it never starts printing, but if it does, the sound is so different from any other sound in the control room that everyone immediately knows there is an emergency. Not only that, but the printer is also printing out what the emergency is. The message is two-fold: First, whatever the method used, if it is used too often it loses effect, something as simple as a dot matrix printer is effective because it is never used for anything else. Second, dot matrix printers are so old fashioned that people don't think of using them any more – but don't write them off completely, they are useful for the most unlikely of tasks, as are a number of older pieces of hardware that we shall be discussing in Chapter 4.

QUESTIONS TO DISCUSS

An interface is to be designed for use in a school entrance hall as an information system for visitors to the school.

Discuss the implications for the HCI of the types of information which may need to be included as part of the HCI, the types of user that may be using it and the type of HCI that may be used. (8)

< Activity >

Visit a cash dispenser/ATM. Study the HCI. Which of our categories does it fit into? Why is it not typical of that type of HCI? Find other HCI applications that are commonly used in everyday life which fit the different types of HCI and determine why each is used in that particular application.

5. Utilities

The OS for any computer has to have available a number of 'house keeping' types of program in order to ensure that the system remains usable. These are not the sort of programs that you would use to produce something useful, like a word processor which you might use to produce a letter. Word processors are an example of applications software. But if a word processor was being used to type a letter it would become necessary to store the letter on a storage device at some point, which would require a special set of instructions to carry it out. Next time the computer was being used, you may want to retrieve the letter. This will need another set of instructions in order to find the letter and put it in the computer's memory. This time the letter is finished, and you tell the computer to print it out – this will require another set of instructions. You no longer need the letter so you tell the computer to delete it; yet another set of instructions. All these

< Discuss >

Is a spell checker a utility program or a piece of applications software? What about a grammar checker? Can we see a clear division between utilities and applications software? If you were an examiner marking a question that asked for an example of a piece of utility software where would you draw the line between what you would accept and what you would not?

'sets of instructions' are little programs called **utilities**. Utilities are programs that are part of the OS and are used to carry out commonly occurring tasks that the OS is expected to do. There are a whole set of utilities, of which we have three examples above, which can be collectively called **file handlers**. The utility that performs the print routine for the letter is a hardware driver. All the peripherals used in a computer system need drivers, small programs that tell the OS how to control them. We all use virus checkers on our computers in order to identify viruses in files and then to get rid of them. When we want to send a large file as an email attachment we would normally make it smaller so that the transmission is carried out more quickly (compression software). These are all utility programs.

QUESTION:

1 a Explain the use of file handling utility software in a computer system. (4)

b State two other types of utility software and state what they are used for. (6)

Two particular types of utility software are those that allow the backing up of files and the archiving of files.

Backing up is the process of making another copy of a file in case anything adverse happens to the first copy. When considering backup procedures they will be different for every application but a number of points should be thought about:

- who will make the backup (it may be automatic)
- when and how often the backup will be made
- how many copies will be made, on what type of medium, where the copies will be stored
- how long should the copies be kept for.

A different type of backup is an incremental backup. This acknowledges that much of the data will be unchanged from taking one backup to the next. In which case, what is the point in copying all that unchanged data again? An incremental backup only copies the altered data.

Archiving is done in order to save space on the main storage device. Many files will tend to be dormant, in other words they are rarely, if ever, used. All they do is use up space on storage and this results in access to it being slowed down. These redundant files are copied to another medium (often in a compressed form) rather than just erasing them, because they might be necessary in the future. These archive files are not used for backup because, apart from anything else, they are not copies of the original files, they are by definition only those files no longer used, but they may be used for reference for legal reasons or for tax purposes.

END OF CHAPTER QUESTION

1   A business deals with selling building supplies both to the trade and to the general public.

Discuss the requirements of the business for backup and archive files.   (8)

Chapter 3 Data: Its Representation, Structure and Management in Information Systems

1. Number systems

Our standard method of counting involves counting ten digits, the digits 0 to 9 and then going back to the start and putting a 1 in front, giving us 10. Count in units of 1 again, all the way to 19 and then back to the start and put a 2 in front. When we get to 99 we go back to the start in both columns and put a 1 in front to get 100, and so on. This, counting in 10s, leads to us calling our number system the decimal or denary system. We are so used to it that we believe it is the only one; not so!

If you were in school 50 years ago you would have used the imperial set of measurements of length rather than the decimal one. In the imperial set of measurements 12 inches made 1 foot. This meant that you had to count to 11 and it then became 1 foot 0 inches. This was a number system based on 12. 3 feet made 1 yard. This meant that you would count to 2 feet and then it would become 1 yard 0 feet. This was a number system based on 3. 220 yards made 1 furlong so from 219 yards you would go to 1 furlong 0 yards. This is a number system based on 220. Finally there were 8 furlongs in a mile so after 7 furlongs would come 1 mile 0 furlongs. This is based on 8.

In one system we had to use number systems based on 12, 3, 220 and 8. It is very confusing to us because the decimal system only uses 10s and powers of 10, but when you had to use them you got very used to it and it was as easy to convert inches to feet to yards as it is to change millimetres to centimetres to metres.

We use lots of different number systems all the time, for example 60 seconds in a minute, 60 minutes in an hour, 24 hours in a day, 7 days in a week… How about base 6 for the number of balls bowled in a given number of overs in cricket?

Computers find it easy to work with a number system based on 2 because only the digits 0 and 1 are used. This means that no electricity flowing down a wire can be represented by a 0 and a 1 can be represented by electricity in the wire. This system is called the binary system. Each digit is a binary digit which is usually shortened to 'bit'.

< Discuss >

Different number bases apart from 10 arise in many places and we are so used to using them we don't think about it (when was the last time you bought half a dozen eggs?). Discuss the different number systems that are commonly used. Is it a coincidence that many of them are based around 6 or a multiple of 6? What do the ancient Babylonians have to do with it?

< Activity >

Find out why the statement in the last paragraph is a little too simplified and that the reality is rather different.

There are computers that can work in different number bases. How do they vary the signals so that they can represent more than 0 and 1?

Try to find out about computers that are not digital computers working in the binary system.

To change a number from our system to base 2 or binary is easy if you use a column diagram.

In junior school we used to put sums in columns with headings on them:

Thousands	Hundreds	Tens	Units

These headings are used because we are in denary (decimal) and so we go up by multiplying the heading by 10 every time. In binary we do the same except the headings go up by multiplying by 2 each time so the column diagram looks like this:

128	64	32	16	8	4	2	1

To turn a denary number into a binary number simply put 1s in each column that is needed to make the number.

For example 75 is 1 lot of 64, 1 lot of 8, 1 lot of 2 and 1 lot of 1, so we get:

128	64	32	16	8	4	2	1
0	1	0	0	1	0	1	1

so 75 in base 10 is equal to 01001011 in binary.

Notice the leading 0. It is usual to work in groups of 8 bits for reasons that we shall understand shortly, so the extra 0s have to be put in. We shall be lazy and say that a group of 8 bits is called a **byte**. A byte is actually something a little different but we shall find that out in a little while; for the moment it is 8 bits.

If the column headings are changed so that we have base 8 numbers it becomes:

512	64	8	1

and using the same principle as for binary:

75 in denary is 1 lot of 64, 1 lot of 8 and 3 ones, so 75 in denary is 0113 in base 8. Base 8 has a special name and it is **octal**.

It gets worse!!!

Some information is stored in computers as numbers in base 16. This base is called **hexadecimal**, or sometimes just **hex**. The principles are exactly the same as for denary, binary or octal (or any other base) except that this one looks worse. If you have to be able to count from 0 to fifteen before going back to the start and putting a 1 in front of the 0 to stand for sixteen it means we have to have sixteen digits. We have ten of them (from 0 to 9) but we need six extra ones. They are the capital letters from A to F.

A stands for the denary value ten

B stands for   eleven

C stands for   twelve

D stands for   thirteen

E stands for   fourteen

F stands for   fifteen

and then 10 (in hex) stands for sixteen (in denary).

The column headings will be:

256	16	1

and 75 will be 4 lots of 16 and 11 ones, so 75 in denary is equal to 4B in hex.

Some numbers look like numbers but do not behave like numbers. A loaf of bread has a bar code number that is used to identify it. A jar of jam has a bar code that identifies it. If we add the two bar codes together do we get the bar code for a jam sandwich? No, because addition of bar codes is meaningless. They do not behave the same way that proper numbers do, even if they look like numbers. Consequently, it is not sensible to treat them as numbers in the normal way.

There is another representation that is very similar to binary that we need to know about, which is called **binary coded decimal** (BCD). It simply represents the different digits in the 'number' separately, using four binary digits for each denary digit.

7 in binary is no eights, 1 four, 1 two and 1 one. That makes 0111.

5 in binary is no eights, 1 four, no twos and 1 one. That makes 0101.

So 75 in BCD is 01110101 (just put the two lots of binary together).

< Discuss >

What is the connection between binary and octal, and between binary and hexadecimal? Try writing the answers to some more denary number conversions in pairs of binary and octal and then binary and hex. Discuss anything that you notice.

< Activity >

BCD is used for holding numeric values and for doing arithmetic with them. This is not part of the specification but might be an interesting exercise.

Try changing 28 and 39 into BCD values. Then try adding the binary together (described later in this section) and explain the answer that is achieved. Can you come up with a rule that will allow addition to be done? (Hint: one method is called 'excess three'). How about subtraction?

Is it worth it?

We have learned how to store numbers in binary form, but we cannot store negatives or fractions yet.

Let's start with negative numbers and go back to the basic method for storing a binary number in 8 bits.

128	64	32	16	8	4	2	1

The reason that we cannot store negative numbers is that there is nowhere to put a minus sign. Easy to solve, just make the first bit stand for either + or -.

+/-	64	32	16	8	4	2	1

So -75 becomes the same as +75 was but with a 1 in the first bit to stand for a – sign.

+/-	64	32	16	8	4	2	1
1	1	0	0	1	0	1	1

This is called 'sign/magnitude representation' because the byte is in two parts: the sign and the size of the number.
So -75 = 11001011.

There are two problems with sign and magnitude. The first is that the biggest number that can be represented is now half what it was (127 instead of 255) and the second is that the binary now contains two types of data: a sign and a value. This means that it becomes very difficult to do arithmetic because different bits mean different things.

Another way of doing negative numbers, which gets round the problem of having a bit that is no longer a number is to use a system called 2s complement. In 2s complement, the first bit stands for -128 instead of just a minus sign, so the diagram looks like this:

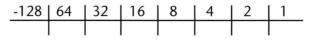

-128	64	32	16	8	4	2	1

Now, -75 must start with a 1 because it is the only place where it can get the minus sign from, but -128 is 53 too many.

So, as well as 1 lot of -128 we will need +53 to get back to -75.

+53 = 1 lot of 32, 1 lot of 16, 1 lot of 4 and a 1. So -75 becomes:

-128	64	32	16	8	4	2	1
1	0	1	1	0	1	0	1

So -75 in 2s complement binary is 10110101.

2s complement becomes very useful when it is necessary to do addition and subtraction because all that needs to be done is to add the bytes together; the minus sign will look after itself!

We will look at fractions in Chapter 16.1.

Let's now look at addition and subtraction.

Addition first:

One of the reasons why computers are designed to use binary is that addition is so simple in binary, much easier than the denary that you are used to. To do denary addition you have to know 100 different addition sums off by heart from 0+0 = 0 to 9+9 = 18. With binary there are only 4 possible sums:

$0 + 0 = 0$

$0 + 1 = 1$

$1 + 0 = 1$

$1 + 1 = 0$, carry 1

Try to follow this addition: 75 + 14

	-128	64	32	16	8	4	2	1	
75 =	0	1	0	0	1	0	1	1	
14 =	0	0	0	0	1	1	1	0	
	0	1	0	1	1	0	0	1	= 89
Carry				1	1	1			

Notice that in the 8s column the sum is 1 + 1 and then a carry is added. Think of it as 1 + 1 = 10 and then add the carry making 11, which is 1 down and carry 1 again.

How about subtraction? Easy if we are using 2s complement because 75 -14 is the same as 75 + (-14). (Remember that -14 is 1 lot of -128 +114).

	-128	64	32	16	8	4	2	1	
75 =	0	1	0	0	1	0	1	1	
-14 =	1	1	1	1	0	0	1	0	
	0	0	1	1	1	1	0	1	= 61
Carry	1				1				

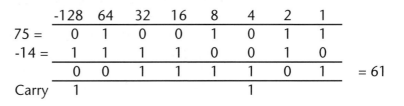

Notice two things: nowhere have we done any subtraction, it's all addition and note that we have ignored the final carry – it disappeared out of the byte so is not part of the answer.

< Activity >

When you are used to doing subtractions try these questions:

14 – 75; 75 + 75; - 75 – 75.

What is the problem?

Can you devise rules by which the computer will be able to predict whether the answer to the sum will be right or wrong?

A computer that is limited in this way is obviously going to be pretty useless. What can be done to improve things?

QUESTION:

1 a Work out the binary equivalents of these denary numbers:

   (i) 39 (ii) 58 (iii) 23
   (iv) 97 (v) 43 (vi) 94

b For the same numbers in part **a** calculate:

   (i) their octal representations
   (ii) their hexadecimal representations
   (iii) their BCD representations.

c Work out the 2s complement and sign magnitude representations of:

   (i) -39 (ii) -58 (iii) -23
   (iv) -97 (v) -43 (vi) -94

d Use the values obtained for binary and 2s complement representations in parts **a** and **c** to work out the following sums. (Show your working. Note: in an exam the bulk of the marks are for the representations and the carries).

   (i) 97 + 23 (ii) 97 – 23
   (iii) 43 + 58 (iv) 43 – 58
   (v) -39 + 43 (vi) 39 – 43

Another type of data that must be stored is text. As an author types in the text of a book, the characters that they are typing must be stored somewhere. We have an idea that the data in a computer must be stored in binary so presumably the characters that are being typed must also be in binary. To distinguish them from numeric data we will call them binary codes.

So, the first question to ask is how many binary codes do we need?

The author needs the letters of the alphabet and their capitals (52) and some punctuation and a few extra ones; let's say an extra 11. That makes 63 altogether and they can get 63 different binary codes by using 6 bits for each character. All that is needed is to decide which character for each code. Let's use 011011 to stand for 'A' and ...

This is all very well, but unless you made the same decisions for your computer, our machines cannot communicate with each other. This was the situation in the early 1960s when the manufacturers of computers realised that this had to be standardised and a meeting was held in America to sort it out. At that meeting a set of codes was decided on so that all computers used the same codes and could talk to each other. This standard was called the ASCII set of codes. It uses 8 bits to stand for each character and 'A' is represented by 01000001 and 'B' by 01000010 and so on.

The fact that 8 bits represent a character is the reason why a byte normally has 8 bits in it. Things can be different, some character sets have more or less characters in them than in ASCII so these computers would use a different size of byte.

< Activity >

ASCII actually represents 127 characters in its character set so why do we need 8 bits per character and not 7? Try to work it out. The answer will become more obvious in Chapter 5.

There is another version of ASCII that has more unusual characters in it and it needs even more bits.

Think about the characters used at an ATM and try to work out its character set and the size of byte that it would use.

How does a computer sort a list of names into alphabetical order? How does it deal with a mixture of capital and lower case letters?

EBCDIC and UNICODE are simply other character sets used in computing.

EBCDIC is nothing to worry about, it is simply a different set of codes. It is used on IBM machines and was originally developed for use on their peripheral devices. It is based on BCD, the coding being done in groups of 4 bits. 'A' is the first character stored in group 12 so it would be represented as 1100 0001.

UNICODE is another set of character codes, very similar to ASCII, except that it contains far more characters. It is designed to include all the symbols that are used throughout the world including all the Arabic and Chinese and Japanese characters. It is constantly growing in size as more and more characters are accepted.

2. Data capture, presentation and entry (including validation and verification of data)

All computing involves the storage and manipulation of data. Before this it is necessary to get the required data into the computer. There are two ways of doing this. The first way is to collect the data in some way that is not connected to the computer and to then type it in using a keyboard.

This is known as a manual method and will involve some kind of data capture form or questionnaire to collect the data. The form must be designed carefully to ensure that it will collect the required data and that it is in no way ambiguous.

For example:

Dates must have completion areas clearly labelled. 01/02/03 means something different depending on the part of the world in which you live. In Britain it means the 1st of February 2003 (or should it be 1903?) and in USA it means 2nd of January 2003. When designing a data capture form the rule must be to take nothing for granted.

It is quite possible to direct the responder by using tick boxes to allow the responder to choose from a number of options or to give a score out of 10 or something similar, but questions on data capture forms should have a limited number of responses, in general, otherwise they cannot be automatically manipulated when in the computer.

Imagine the question, 'How well do you think the Government is doing?'

If you asked 1000 people that question as part of an opinion poll you would probably get 1000 different answers because people would express themselves in different ways. On the other hand, if you gave 3 possible responses to tick: 'Well', 'Alright', 'Badly', then the computer can add up the responses and give an indication of how the population thinks the Government is doing.

Other considerations are centred on persuading people to actually fill in the form. The form should not be too long or people will not bother; there should be instructions about what is required and it should look official.

When the forms are returned to the organisation they must be input to the computer system. Someone reading the data direct from the forms will probably type in the data direct to the computer. There are a number of ways that the data that ends up in the computer can be wrong. We will take as an example a date of birth that is on the form as 01/02/03 (meaning the first of February 2003).

< Discuss >

Think about the design of a data capture form to be sent to parents of children due to start at the school the following September. Consider what type of data capture is required, what the style of the questions should be, and how the parent is going to respond to the questions. What other information needs to be either on the form or sent with the form?

When this is typed in the typist may have hit the wrong key and it goes into the machine as 41/02/03. This is obviously wrong because months cannot have 41 days in them. This data entered has broken a rule. As long as the computer knows what the rules are it can tell the operator that it has been entered wrongly and to correct it. When the computer knows the rule and can check it, it is known as **data validation**.

This type of data validation is known as a **range check** because it checks that the data is within a certain range, in this case between 1 and 31 (or 1 and 28 if it is a bit more sophisticated).

Other validation checks are:

1 A **format check:** 01/02/003 would be rejected because the computer knows the format should be xx/xx/xx and will not accept anything else.
2 A **length check:** 01/02/003 will be rejected because the computer knows to expect 8 characters and it got 9.
3 A **character check:** a1/02/03 will be rejected because the computer knows the first character has to be a digit.
4 A **presence check:** the typist missed it out, the computer will report an error because it was expecting data.

What about if the typist types in 11/02/03? This passes all the rules so the computer will not spot the error. This could be spotted with a 'visual check' of the data as it comes up on the screen, or if it was very important data, it could be entered twice and the computer could check that the entries are the same – any difference would mean that an error had been made. This is called 'double entry' of the data. The computer is verifying that the data has been entered correctly and this is called **data verification**.

What about the date being typed in as 01/02/03 when it should have been typed in as 02/02/03? This is an error that is not going to be discovered by data entry techniques.

Other methods of data input are automatic data input methods. These are where the data is collected in such a way that it is input to the computer as it is collected. In some automatic data collection methods the data is input as it arises, with no special preparation. Examples would be speech input and physical data collected by sensors, like temperature. Speech is interpreted by comparing the sounds that are input with stored data. This does mean that input can be temperamental. Physical data is collected by sensors and fed into the computer via a device that turns the measurement into a binary signal (an analogue to digital converter) without any human intervention. If the data is physical there will be a sensor that is capable of measuring it.

< Discuss >

Discuss rules that could be given to the computer system so that the data input from your form can be validated on input.

There are two other types of data validation that will be introduced later in this section.

Some automatic data capture and input requires that the data is in a particular form before it is read.

A bar code reader reads the light and dark parallel lines on many products and devices, but the bar code has had to be created first. The dark lines are read in pairs and correspond to digits that combine to form the bar code that will convey information about the article to the computer.

< Activity >

We all know of the use of bar codes in supermarkets, but find out what other uses there are for them. Where can they be used in schools and what is the data being represented?

Optical Mark Recognition (OMR) is the use of shading in of boxes or specific areas of a form to represent data. In this case it is not the shading in of the area that conveys the data, but the position of the shading. Imagine a lottery ticket. The boxes are shaded in according to the numbers chosen; if the shading is in a different position then different numbers are chosen. Consequently, the positioning of the paper for reading must be precise.

Optical Character Reading (OCR) is the reading of the shapes of the individual characters by the computer and these shapes are then compared to standard shapes of characters stored in the computer's memory. A good example is when type written documents need to be read into the computer system so that they can be edited using a piece of word processing software.

Magnetic Ink Character Recognition (MICR) is when characters are printed on documents in magnetisable ink to prepare them for reading into the computer in future. The ink can be magnetised, which means that the characters are more likely to be read accurately by the computer. A typical use is on some passport documents.

< Discuss >

Discuss and collect different applications that use the three types of data input mentioned on this page. Note particularly the difference between OMR and OCR.

Find out how the data is read from each of the source documents.

Notice that the three methods mentioned above are different from bar codes in that they are not only computer readable, but the information is also readable by humans.

Cameras, both video and electronic still cameras, can be used to capture images which can then be manipulated, composed and output by a computer.

< Activity >

Describe the image capture and the processing which will be carried out when a fairground ride takes pictures of the people on it and then allows them to be processed to appear on various souvenirs that can be purchased.

< Discuss >

Think about the example of the weather station and discuss the following:

- the equipment that would be necessary
- the sensors needed and how they would work
- the method of storing the data collected, including the timings of when the data should be collected
- how the data collected can be sent to the meteorological offices.

A weather station is situated on the uninhabited isle of Rockall. It is intended that various instruments will be used to automatically measure the rainfall, the wind speed and direction, the temperature and the hours of sunshine.

< Activity >

Following the discussion write a report for the meteorological service, saying how the equipment could provide information to help the process of weather forecasting.

3. Outputs from a system

A computer game consists of driving a car around a motor racing circuit. The player can use different gears, different amounts of acceleration and braking. The condition of the car is shown on the screen and the player can pause the game at the end of each lap and bring up a record of the decisions that were made during the previous lap.

The forms that the output for this game will probably take will be:

- video, so that a realistic view of the race is on the screen
- sound, to provide atmosphere and clues as to the performance of the engine
- graphical images, to show the map of the track and your position on it and also the dials showing speed and time
- tabular information, to show the salient points from the last lap
- text, to report on any problems that may arise
- some form of alarm to warn when fuel is low.

These different forms of output are all designed to give information for different reasons.

< Discuss >

Discuss the different forms of output that would be effective in educational software aimed at teaching:

- different subjects
- different age groups.

END OF CHAPTER QUESTION

1   Discuss the need for different types of hard copy output depending on the type of application requiring the output.   (8)

Further examples of appropriate output formats and their links with the study of the HCI are considered in Unit 2.

Chapter 4 Hardware

1. Processor components

The processor is the central part of a computer. It is sometimes called the **central processing unit** (CPU). It normally consists of some special registers, the Arithmetic Logic Unit (ALU) and the Control Unit (CU). It usually also includes the main memory or Immediate Access Store (IAS).

The CU manages the execution of instructions. It fetches the instruction, decodes it and synchronises its execution. It then sends control signals to other parts of the processor in order that the instructions are carried out. These signals are communicated around the processor using pathways (like mini cables) called busses. There are different types of busses that differ depending on the type of data that they are expected to communicate. The CU uses a bus called the control bus to send commands to different parts of the processor.

The data and instructions are both stored in the main memory of the computer and any arithmetic instructions are carried out in the ALU, as are any logical comparisons. The ALU also acts as the gateway to the processor, all inputs and outputs having to pass through it before being directed to other parts of the processor or computer system.

The special registers keep a check on the progress of the instructions and data as they move around the processor. They appear to be daunting, but they are actually very straightforward to understand if they are thought of as a part of a logical operation rather than as individual registers. The registers are presented here in the logical order in which they occur in the process:

- **Program counter** (PC): keeps a check on whereabouts the next instruction is in the memory. This means that after one instruction has been carried out the PC will always be able to tell the processor where the next instruction is. The number in there is incremented every time it is read and the instructions are always stored in order so it is read, and then immediately is set to point to the next instruction.
- **Memory address register** (MAR): this is where the address that was read from the PC is sent. It is stored in here so that the processor knows whereabouts in the memory the instruction is.
- **Memory data register** (MDR): the memory is searched to find the address that is being held in the MAR and whatever is in that address must be the instruction. A copy of it is placed in the MDR.

- **Current instruction register** (CIR): the instruction that is now in the MDR is copied into the CIR. When it is in the CIR, the instruction can be split into its parts. One part is sent to the computer to be decoded so that the processor knows what sort of instruction it is, and so that it can send signals to the relevant parts of the processor to carry out the instructions. Another part is an address that tells the processor whereabouts in the memory the data is that is to be used. So if the instruction is ADD 20, it will be split up, the control unit works out how to do an 'add', and the 20 is where the processor will find the data that has to be added.
- The address part (20 in our example) is sent back to the MAR.
- The memory is then searched and whatever is in the address 20 is copied into the MDR.
- The value in the MDR can then be used according to the instruction in the CIR.
- If the instruction is to do some arithmetic or logical comparison the data is sent to the Accumulator that will carry out the task.

< Activity >

Some things to think about:

- Try to find out what a Memory buffer register is.
- If 010 means ADD when it is decoded and 101 means SUBTRACT when it is decoded, then explain what 10101001 means if it is an instruction.
- What will be the difference between ADD and SUBTRACT?
- Try to come up with a list of sensible instructions that a computer should be able to recognise.

Much of the last few pages have been about sending signals around the processor. We have already said that one bus is the control bus that sends instructions from the control unit to different parts of the processor. There are two other busses that we should know about:

- the data bus, which carries the data from one register to another
- the address bus, which carries the location address to which the data is going.

As they travel around the processor the various localities look at the address as it passes and if it matches then the data is grabbed.

The memory of a computer can have different characteristics and computers need to have all of them in differing amounts. The two main characteristics are the ability to store data when the power is switched off and the ability to change data that is stored there. These two characteristics describe the two main types of memory perfectly. One is called Read Only Memory (ROM) and as the

< Discuss >

Imagine a processor controlling a central heating system. Discuss the memory requirements of the system. How would they differ from the requirements of a personal computer?

name implies, data that is held on here cannot be altered. The data is not erased when the power is switched off, which makes it ideal for storing the instructions that a computer needs to 'boot' itself into life when the power is switched back on again. This program is called the boot (or bootstrap) program. There are many other programs or parts of programs that may be on the ROM of a computer but the boot program is the only one that is certainly there. The second type is called Random Access Memory (RAM) and is characterised by the fact that the data is wiped clear when the power is switched off. This sounds like a negative thing, but it isn't. If there was no memory that could be altered then the computer would only ever be able to do one thing and no instructions could be given to it. The quality of being erasable when power is lost is called being 'volatile' while ROM is 'non-volatile'.

< Activity >

Try to find out what is meant by the BIOS. Where is the BIOS stored? Why is it unreasonable to think of the BIOS being stored in ROM or in RAM?

Research into other types of memory and create a table of their characteristics. Some to get you started are PROM, EPROM and SDRAM.

Figure 1.1 Bar code

Figure 1.2 OMR is used for lottery tickets

2. Peripheral devices

There are three types of peripheral device:

- input
- output
- storage.

Some, like touch screens, can be more than one type at the same time, but most fall neatly into one of the three categories.

Input devices

We have mentioned some of these already in Chapter 3 when talking about methods of inputting data into computer systems, but now we need to talk about the hardware items that actually do it.

In Chapter 3 we talked about bar code reading and the fact that the bars on bar codes, taken in pairs, can stand for numbers which, put together, can make a code which stands for something. That is all very well, but if it is going to be useful we need a machine that can read the bars. The shining of a laser at the bars does this and the difference in light reflection between the light and dark bars is information that the computer can then use. The same sort of thing is true for OCR and OMR, as they both recognise marks on the paper document. OMR is very like the bar code reader except that an OM reader shines light at the page and recognises where on the page the marks have been made. In this case different positions stand for different things. Most documents that are used in OMR are printed using light blue or pink ink. This is deliberate; special ink that does not show up under the light is used, meaning that, apart from the marks on the page the page looks blank. OCR is similar except that a scan is made of the whole page and the different shapes of characters are then compared with shapes in the memory to determine what is printed on the page.

Notice that these are all optical devices of some sort; the same would be true of a scanner and to a lesser extent of a digital camera. These devices work by dividing the page or picture into a grid of small squares, each of which is then studied by shining light onto it and noting its reflection. A value is then given to it. In the simplest case the value for each square will be a 0 or a 1. Consider the picture of a dog with the grid lines superimposed over it.

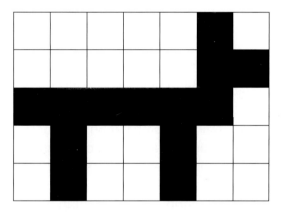

Figure 1.3

This dog would be stored in the computer as:
0000010000001111111001001000100100

Admittedly, the dog is not brilliant and you need to screw your eyes up to be able to see it, but the principle is reasonable. The image can be improved simply by increasing the number of squares (called pixels) used. The higher the number of pixels, the better (or 'higher') the resolution of the image. The other way of improving the image is to increase the number of colours. At the moment we only have black and white and this means that a 0 or 1 can represent each of the pixels. If we expand the number of bits used to represent each pixel to 2 we can now represent shades of grey. 00 is white, 01 is light grey, 10 is dark grey and 11 is black. If each pixel is represented by an 8 bit byte then 256 different shades can be represented and a good quality monochrome picture can be achieved. Colour is more difficult. Each pixel needs a combination of 3 colours: red, green and blue, in the same way that a colour television picture is made up of three base colours. However, each of the three base colours will require a byte per pixel, so each pixel will need a minimum of 3 bytes. A picture with a million pixels will need 3 million bytes or 3 Megabytes of memory to store it. This large storage requirement has made the storage of high definition colour images difficult in the past but storage is now so plentiful that these problems have been overcome. Video pictures have similar storage problems, but this is exacerbated because they are reliant on a large number of images that need to be refreshed in quick succession.

< Activity >

In Chapter 2.5 we mentioned a number of different pieces of utility software, one of which was compression software. Using the picture of the dog as a starting point try to describe different ways of compressing data while still maintaining the information contained.

< Discuss >

Discuss the advantages and disadvantages of these different types of input devices, paying particular attention to problems that may arise with each.

These methods of input all depend, to a greater or lesser extent, on optical means of input, but MICR is read differently. The data is printed onto the document using ink that can be magnetised. The Magnetic Ink Character Reader then scans the document and picks up the magnetic pulses from the characters, making the reading of the characters more accurate.

More common than any of these devices is the keyboard and mouse combination that most of us use. The computer keyboard contains a number of characters with each key on the keyboard corresponding to a specific combination of 0s and 1s that identify the key that has been pressed. The mouse works by recognising quantity of movement in two axes; think of them like the x and y axes in graphs. It sends messages to the computer to say how many units it has been pushed in each direction. The computer can then translate this into movement of a pointer (cursor) up and down the screen.

< Activity >

Compare the keys on the keyboard with a set of characters that are recognised in ASCII. Many more characters than this are available to the user of the keyboard, so where do they come from? Are they stored in ASCII form? Find an old keyboard that does not work properly any more. Cut through the wire used to connect it to the computer. Work out a connection between the number of characters on a keyboard, the number of characters in ASCII and the wire that you have exposed. What other controls are available on a mouse? How are these different controls made available to the user? How does a mouse work (both those that have a mouse ball and those that are laser)?

A mouse is typically either connected to the computer by a cable or by a wireless connection. Many devices are connected to the computer by a cable, and this is known as hard wiring. There are many different types of wiring that can be used, ranging from simple copper cable to optic fibre using light rather than electricity.

< Activity >

Each of these means of cabling have their own advantages and disadvantages but they do not concern us here, however it may be an interesting exercise to go on the internet and look up CAT5 cable to get a feel of the types of characteristic that can be generally thought important.

Figure 1.4 Touch Screen

Some use wireless communication to send data from one part of a system to another and while there are great benefits to be had from not being tied down to a physical locality in order to use the cable, there are significant problems with lack of privacy. The lack of privacy is caused by the fact that if data is being broadcast it is difficult to ensure that the data only goes to one recipient.

There are many other input devices that are designed for specific uses. A microphone is an input device that collects sound and can input it to a system. The sound collected does not need to be a voice, although it may be. For instance a microphone provides one of the inputs to the burglar alarm system on a car. It listens for the sound of broken glass and if that sound is detected the processor will set off the alarm because one of the windows may have been broken. A touch screen is an interesting device in that it allows the user to input the data while having no technological knowledge above the ability to point at the screen.

< Activity >

Try to find out how the system finds out whereabouts the user is pointing on the screen.

< Discuss >

Why should a touch screen be called 'both an output and input device', rather than input and output?

This means that touch screens are largely vandal proof and can be exposed to the elements in places such as train stations in order to act as information boards. In order to give a sensible input, the user needs information to be output to the screen which makes the touch screen a rather unique peripheral device in that it acts as both an output and input device.

< Activity >

Some cars have automatic windscreen wipers. Decide what input is needed to this system to allow it to work and investigate what peripherals are used to provide the required input.

Chapter 4 Hardware

37

< Discuss >

Discuss the other factors that can contribute to a decision about the monitor that is used for different applications (use the details of different monitors that can be found on websites and try to link them to suitable applications according to their characteristics).

Output devices

Output devices can be split into two types:

- those that give a hard copy printout
- those that are soft copy.

Hard copy is basically anything that you can take away from the machine and that will last for some time. Typical hard copy devices are printers because the output is on a piece of paper while soft copy devices are typified by monitor screens where the output is lost every time it needs to be replaced by another screen. Monitors are characterised by physical qualities such as whether they are flat screen or tube-driven, and also by their size. They are also characterised according to their picture quality, which is largely dependent on the number of pixels that can be shown on the screen. The physical characteristics are probably more important nowadays. If there is a limited amount of space on the receptionist's desk then it is important to use a flat screen monitor. If the receptionist is a bit short-sighted then that may be a reason for using a 17" monitor rather than a 12" one, despite the size of the desk.

Figure 1.5 Laser printer

Printers are hard copy devices. Whatever the method of producing the hard copy they all have that one thing in common – an output that is permanent and can be taken away. There are almost as many different types of printer as there are applications for which they are used. Currently, the most common types of printer in use are laser and inkjet printers. Laser printers work by a laser beam being directed onto a rotating drum. The laser is switched on and off very quickly, producing a series of pulses that are directed onto the surface of the drum. Where the laser light hits the drum it becomes charged. The drum rotates through a trough of toner and the toner sticks to the areas of the drum that are charged. The paper is then pressed against the surface of the drum and the toner is transferred to the paper. Notice that the characters produced are really a set of dots, but we should expect that because that is how they are produced in the computer. Colour laser printers work in exactly the same way except that the process is repeated four times, once for each of the three colours (actually cyan, magenta and yellow and then a fourth time for black). Another type of printer is an inkjet printer. Inkjets work by squirting ink at the paper. If the ink is squirted accurately enough and sparingly enough then characters can be formed on the paper. Again, different coloured inks in four syringes can produce colour images and black. These two printers are both known as non-impact printers because the mechanism does not involve the use of pressure.

A dot matrix printer is an impact printer that works by forcing pins against an inked ribbon that, in turn, presses against the paper, leaving a dot. This is a mechanical process and, as such, it is slower than a non-impact system, and the images are of lower resolution. The benefit of impact printers, however, is that they can impact on more than one sheet of paper at a time, thus making more than one copy of a printout and this is useful if the organisation wishes to keep a copy and also give the customer a copy. Another type of printer that must be mentioned is a plotter. This is a specialised type of printer that works by having a pen move up and down a gantry over the paper while the gantry moves in the perpendicular axis up and down the paper. The pen can be lifted from or put onto the surface of the paper to produce the printout. These are particularly used for producing things like architects' drawings.

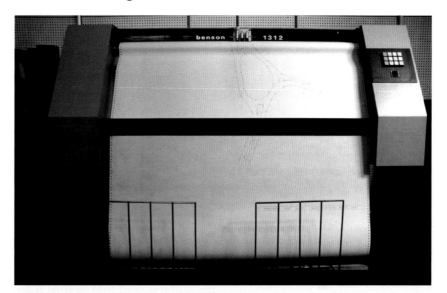

Figure 1.6 Flat bed plotter

< Activity >

Find out about other types of printer. You could start with flat bed and drum plotters and then go on to bubblejet, chemical and other printers. For each type of printer try to establish a particular area in which it would be useful and decide which of its characteristics make it suitable for your chosen use.

Storage devices

It is more accurate to refer to these as secondary storage devices because we are not looking at the internal memory storage of the computer, but to the types of storage device that can be added to the computer to make it function more efficiently. Storage devices can be categorised into one of three types:

- magnetic
- optical
- solid state.

Magnetic devices are typified by the hard disk that is part of most computers. It is misnamed because it will consist of a series of disks

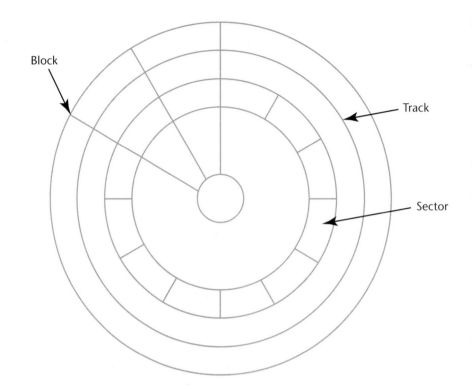

Block

Track

Sector

Figure 1.7 Surface of a disk

< Discuss >

Why is the index track the middle track? How does the indexing work? Where does the indexing of the sectors start from? How does the indexing of one set of data spread over a number of blocks work?

called a platter, stored on top of each other, each having its own read/write head. This not only increases the volume of data that can be stored but also the speed of access to the data. The data is stored as small amounts of magnetism on the surface of the disks that can be read by the heads and can then be interpreted as standing for a 0 or a 1. The technology has not altered much in 30 years, but what has altered is the density with which the data can be packed onto the surface, and that in turn means that more data can be stored and can be retrieved more easily. The surface of the disk is capable of storing so much data that there needs to be a way of finding it. The surface is divided into a series of concentric rings, called **tracks**, and the tracks are further divided into smaller areas called **blocks** by lines radiating out from the centre forming cheese shaped wedges called **sectors**. The central track is used as an index track so that data stored in the blocks can be found easily. If the data is too big to fit into one block then the blocks are linked until there is enough space for the data. This division of the surfaces of the disks needs to be done by the operating system because it will be different for different machines. This process is called **formatting** a disk and it is carried out by a piece of utility software called the **disk formatter**.

The other type of magnetic secondary storage is **magnetic tape**. This is old technology but is still used widely, particularly for archiving files. The basic difference between tape and disk storage is that data stored on a tape is stored linearly along the surface of the tape. This means that, although the volumes that can be stored are enormous, the access times are very slow because access relies on the system finding the correct position on the tape and this can only be done by 'fast forwarding' to the correct position.

< Activity >

< Discuss >

What are the differences between a CD and a DVD and what is the difference between a medium and a drive?

Optical devices are typified by **CDs** and **DVDs**. They have a number of similarities with hard drives. The surface is divided into sectors and a (single) track. The track is a spiral, similar to that found on a vinyl record. The data is stored in the sectors and on the track. Small indentations are made in the surface of the disk. A laser is aimed at the disk surface and where there is no indentation the laser light is focused in such a way that it will simply disperse. However, where there is an indentation the laser light has to travel a greater distance, far enough for the light to become focused so that when it is reflected it is reflected into the sensor. Again, this gives two states that can stand for 0 and 1. It is important to note that the distinction between CDs and DVDs is not really important to our work as it just reflects a difference in scale. However, the distinction between a CD and a CD-RW is very important. There is no point in giving an answer of a CD to a question that asks for a medium on which to store a backup, because you may not be able to write onto it, so be careful.

Solid-state storage is typically found in flash memory or your USB stick. It has no moving parts, so it is different from the other two types because there is no mechanical process involved. The data is stored in a thin layer of oxide between two non-conductive layers. The data in the oxide layer can be altered by sending pulses of power to the different, tiny areas in that layer. Further information can be gleaned from websites, particularly www.howstuffworks.com, though be aware that the information contained is far too advanced for this course and should only be for interest's sake. In this course, we are far more interested in when and why the different types of storage are used rather than in how they work.

A computer-controlled milking machine is to be installed in a farm to automate the process of milking cows. Suggest a suitable set of peripherals for this application.

This application is somewhat less well defined than it would be in an exam question but it does allow us to think about how to go about answering the question. The first thing to think about is the application. What are its characteristics? The milking parlour is on a farm so it is going to be dirty! The person using the equipment is a farmer, not a computer specialist, so the equipment must be easy to use. The farmer will need to keep records, so we will need to have hard copy as well as secondary storage. The cows will have to be monitored when giving the milk and they will also

< Discuss >

Bearing in mind all the points made about the computer-controlled milking machine, discuss the hardware configuration needed.

have to be identified in order to maintain records about individual cows.

We have discussed how the computer system comprises so many different forms of hardware, but they can only work satisfactorily if they are able to communicate with each other. To understand how this communication is done it is necessary to introduce two new concepts.

Buffers: these are small areas of memory/storage that act to temporarily store data while it is waiting to be used or to be sent somewhere else. A printer will have a buffer whose job is to store the work sent from the processor while the printer prints it out. This lets the processor get on with something else and not have to wait until the printout is finished before it can carry on.

Interrupts: these are messages sent from other places to the processor. There are many types of interrupt which we will meet later, but the need here is for one that can be sent to the processor when the printer runs out of data in the buffer (it's only small) and wants some new data sent so that it can carry on.

There will be questions that arise from this, such as 'If more than one interrupt comes at once how does the system know what to do first?' (Chapter 13.2) or 'If a job gets interrupted, how does it get back to it in the right place?' (Chapter 15). Hopefully any other questions will come up in later units. (If they are answered later then it means you don't need to worry about them here!)

END OF CHAPTER QUESTIONS

1 a Describe how:
    (i)   MICR   (2)
    (ii)   OCR   (2)
    are used to input data to a computer system.
  b (i)   State an application for which the use of OMR as an input method would be appropriate.   (1)
    (ii)   Explain why OMR is appropriate for the application you have chosen.   (3)
(OCR AS Computing paper 2506 – June 2006)

2 Describe the purpose of the:
    (i)   control unit
    (ii)   memory unit
    (iii) Arithmetic logic unit
    as individual parts of a processor.   (6)
(OCR AS Computing paper 2506 – June 2006)

3 a State what is meant by:
    (i)   hardware
    (ii)   software
    in a computer system.   (2)
  b Explain why a storage device is needed on most computer systems.   (2)
(OCR AS Computing paper 2506 – June 2006)

4 a Explain the difference between RAM and ROM. (2)

 b State two types of data stored in the RAM of a personal computer system, other than the user
   data files. (2)

 c Give one advantage and one disadvantage of storing the operating system in ROM. (2)

(OCR AS Computing paper 2506 – June 2006)

5 A computer system is supplied with two types of secondary storage device: a hard disk drive
  and a DVD rewritable drive.

 a State two types of information that will be stored on each medium. (4)

 b State one other type of secondary storage device that the owner of the system might buy, and give
   a reason why it would be useful. (2)

(OCR AS Computing paper 2506 – June 2006)

Chapter 5 Data Transmission

1. Data transmission

< Discuss >

Under what circumstances does the communication between two computers make sense and under what circumstances will a computer not be sensibly communicating with others?

A computer working by itself is often very useful. A computer-controlled washing machine does not need to be in communication with the computer that controls the tumble drier, or perhaps it does!

However, one of the prime reasons for using a computer is to be able to communicate with others. To be able to send email communications, to send files of data from one place to another, to allow collaboration on projects between people, to ensure that people working in an organisation are not working in a vacuum. For all of these reasons and many more it is important that computers are able to communicate with each other. This means that the data must be able to be sent along cables from one machine to another, or by some other means of communication which may be wireless communication or using fibre optic cables or any of the methods described in Chapter 4.

Computers that are connected together are said to be **networked**. There are two types of network which interest us, a **Local Area Network** (LAN) which is probably what you use at school or if you have a number of computers at home connected via a wireless connection, and a **Wide Area Network** (WAN), the most common one being the Internet. The first difference between them is obvious; the LAN has all the machines close together whereas the WAN tends to be spread more remotely. The LAN is probably hard wired using cable or is connected via a wireless system while the WAN probably uses a communication system that is not owned by the owners of the computers – in the case of using the Internet it would be a telecommunications company like BT. Because the WAN probably uses a public communications medium it is easier to intercept messages, unlike in a LAN where the data is far more secure as long as it is not connected to a WAN like the Internet. These differences are not always true; for instance some organisations, such as banks, control their own means of communication around the network.

A typical network will need something in each computer to allow it to communicate with other machines, some physical means of communication and something to control the communications. Machines will need a device called a **Network Interface Card** (NIC), through which all communication with the network is carried out. This NIC will use a medium, either by being connected to a cable or by being connected to a wireless antenna so that the messages can be passed, and to software that can control the whole process (a Network Operating System (NOS)).

Not only does the network allow communication but it also allows sharing of files, software and hardware (e.g. printers). We do not need a printer for every computer, but rather we can share printers and even ensure that different types of printer are available to the computers. Because the files and the software are being shared it means that at certain times some of the files will be required by many of the machines. This will mean that there may be a lot of traffic on the network (for example at the start of a lesson) and this will cause bottlenecks and slow down the network. Problems like this can be solved in a number of ways. It may be that a change in the way that the network is wired together may be all that is required, although this may mean the use of extra types of hardware.

An alternative is to store files and software at different places on the network so that all the data is not coming from the same place. Ultimately though, the system is going to be reliant on the ability of the hardware to maintain communications and a compromise is usually made between what is practicable and what speeds are acceptable.

Time to consider the messages being transmitted!

We have seen how the data held on computer systems is in the form of binary digits. If data is going to be transmitted then the bits have to be sent from one machine to another.

Consider the 8 bit byte that we have been talking about and imagine it being stored in a part of a computer ready to be sent to another computer:

One way of doing the transmission would be to send the byte, one bit at a time, through a single wire (connection):

This is known as **serial data transmission**.

> < Discuss >

Some extra hardware is usually used in networks. Try to find out about bridges, routers, servers and gateways.

If all the computers in your school were on the same LAN discuss the problems that would arise and how you could solve them.

Another way would be to use a number of wires, one for each of the bits in the byte. This is known as **parallel transmission of data**:

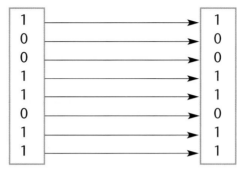

Parallel transmission is much faster than serial transmission but serial transmission is safer because it is difficult to keep all the bits together as they will naturally be transmitted at slightly differing rates.

If the transmission of data is only ever in one direction like the transmission of data from a mouse to a computer, it is known as **simplex data transmission**. Most of the time however, the transmission needs to be in both directions. If it is possible to transmit data in both directions at the same time it is called **duplex** (or full duplex) **transmission**. If, however, the transmission can only be in one direction at a time it is known as **half duplex**.

The more wires connecting two devices, the more data that can be transmitted in a given period of time. The number of bits that can be transmitted in a given period of time is called the **bit rate**. The bit rate is measured in units called **baud** and the 'baud rate' is the number of bits that can be transmitted per second. Low bit rates are obviously of importance in some applications, as are high bit rates, but not perhaps where you would expect it. Take, for example, the transmission of a video from one device to another. Video files are very large volume files so the immediate thought is that it will require a high bit rate for the transmission. However, this is not necessarily true. If the recipient is not going to watch the video until next week then it can take days to download onto the recipient's hard drive; when it is needed it can run straight from the hard drive. However, if the recipient wants to watch the video as it arrives (called **streaming**) the data must arrive quickly enough to stop pausing or the breaking up of the picture or sound. This effect can sometimes be seen on a network if all the machines on a network are being used to watch the same video as it is being streamed around the network. If the picture starts freezing then the bit rate is not high enough to cope. Notice that the problem is not caused by the size of the files being sent, but by the way that the files are to be used. These files are said to be time sensitive because they lose their value unless they arrive in a particular time period.

< Discuss >

Where have we seen parallel and serial data transmission methods being used?

< Discuss >

In Chapter 4 we have discussed the transmission of data to and from different peripheral devices and the primary memory of the computer. Discuss the need for data transmission in this process and which of the different methods introduced in this chapter would be suitable for the process.

< Discuss >

What factors contribute to the bit rate?

Discuss the types of file that require a high bit rate.

When data is transmitted from one location to another it can become corrupted and, put simply, a bit which starts as a 1 may end up as a 0. It is necessary to maintain the integrity of data being transmitted, and procedures need to be used that can check the data received to ensure that it is as it started. There are three methods that we shall look at.

Echoing back: if a set of data is transmitted from one device to another, one checking mechanism is to send it back to the sending device. When the data gets back to the sending device it is compared to what was sent, and if the two sets of data match we can assume that it got there OK. However, if it is different, an error has occurred somewhere, so the original data is sent again. This process is then repeated until the 'echo' matches the original.

Check sums: the data that is sent is made up of binary numbers. Numbers can be added together. When a set of data is sent the original bytes are added together (any carries out of the byte are ignored so that the answer is, itself, a byte), and the answer is then sent with the data. When the data bytes get to the destination they are added together and their 'checksum' is worked out. If the calculated checksum is the same as the one that has been sent it is assumed that the data has not been corrupted; if it is different then the data needs to be resent.

Parity check: data is sent in fixed byte sizes (normally 8 bits). The data being sent would be in the first 7 bits of the byte, the eighth bit being reserved as the parity bit. Imagine that the data is 0110110, and there is one bit left over which is used as the check. The parity check works by making the number of 1s in a byte either always odd or always even. This is something that has to be sorted out during the first contact between the devices, whether they will agree to use odd or even parity checking. If we consider the example given, there are four 1s in the data at the moment. Four is an even number, so if the devices are using even parity the last bit will be set to 0. On the other hand if odd parity is being used then we have to have an odd number of 1s in the byte. The 7 bits we already have cannot be changed because that would change the data, but the eighth bit can be set to 1, giving five 1s, which is odd. So the data above would be sent as 01101100 in a system with even parity and 01101101 in an odd parity system. Whichever parity, the data stays the same and it is the final bit that changes (called the parity bit).

< Activity >

Try to find out if the machine that you are using is using echoing or not.

The problem with parity checking is that it will discover one error in a byte, but if there are two errors resulting from the data transmission the parity check will work and the data will be accepted. For example, odd parity is used and the byte 01101101 is sent. It arrives as 01001101 and an error will be spotted because there are an even number of 1s. But if 00001101 arrives it will be accepted as there is an odd number of 1s. Discuss how this problem can be spotted if the bytes are sent in groups (called blocks) of 7 bytes at a time. (Hint: an eighth byte would also be sent). If an error occurred, is it necessary to send the whole block again? Under what conditions could the block be 'self checking' and when would a resend be necessary?

< Discuss >

Why is the speed of transmission not an advantage of either method of transmission?

2. Circuit switching and packet switching

When data is sent from one machine to another via a network it needs to be collected together into 'bundles' of data called **packets**. It does not matter what the size of the message is; the packets are of a standard size, so bigger messages simply have more packets. Each packet of data has a label attached saying what data file it is part of, which packet it is (numbered in sequence) and where it is going. These packets can then be sent on the network to the destination. There are two ways of sending the data packets across the network: **circuit switching** and **packet switching**. In circuit switching a path between the two machines is established first and all the packets are sent along that path in order. The path is reserved for the duration of the message and is then shut down. This does tie up resources on the network that could probably be used more efficiently, but it does mean that the packets arrive at their destination in the right order. In packet switching the individual packets are sent onto the network to follow the most convenient paths at that time, which means that they end up going by different routes. When a packet reaches a machine on the network the label is read and, if it is not destined for that machine, the most suitable direction available is chosen and the packet is launched down another route. Eventually all the packets will end up at the destination but they will be out of order so the packets have to be rearranged before the file of data is used. Packet switching does not tie up large parts of the network and it makes it very difficult to intercept a message because all the packets follow different routes. Notice that the speed of transmission should not be given as an advantage for either method of transmission.

3. Protocols

A **protocol** is defined as a set of rules, so in this context a protocol is 'a set of rules that govern the transmission of data'. In data transmission the machines involved need to know how they should carry out the task. Earlier in this section we saw the importance of the bit rate used for data transmission, but more important than the type of data to be sent is the requirement that the devices involved should agree on what that bit rate should be. There is no point in one device transmitting at a different rate than the other can receive, because the data pulses will get confused. Part of the protocol must be an agreement over bit rates. Another part will be parity; if the data is sent as having even parity and the receiving device is expecting odd parity, messages will never be accepted. The same goes for echoing back. If one device is set to send back data and the other is not then the data will never be checked. Other important aspects to the protocol would be what character set is used. What type of data transmission is used. What type of medium is used to connect the devices?

The rules that go to make up the protocol are divided into two parts:

- those parts that are logically based
- those that are physically based.

< Discuss >

What is the effect of the protocol on the various pieces of communication hardware, like bridges, that are mentioned in Chapter 5.1?

Explain the need for a handshaking signal and define what it does.

The logical parts can generally be thought of as applying to the data while the physical parts can be thought of as being applied to the methods used for the communication, such as are we going to use cable or wireless? If cable, what sort of cable? If wireless, what frequencies will be used?

In reality this distinction is further split up. This further division is not part of our specification but the different parts of the protocol are arranged in layers. Each layer contains different information. The different types of information about the protocol can be thought of as being reliant on each other, a simple example being that the choice of the physical means of communication will dictate whether it is possible to use serial or parallel transmission of the data. Because there is a sensible structure of one thing having to be decided before going on to the next it allows us to put the various layers in order and it means that changes to the protocol can be made easily by altering just one layer and the links to the other layers it is in contact with, not the whole protocol. This has meant a standardisation of the components of a computer system.

4. Networking

Networking is covered in all areas of this chapter as data transmission is precisely what networking is.

END OF CHAPTER QUESTIONS

1 a Explain what is meant by a protocol. (2)

   b When data is transmitted from one device to another, errors can occur in the transmitted data.
      Explain how parity bits and checksums can be used to detect transmission errors. (6)

   (OCR AS Computing paper 2506 – Jun 2006)

2 a Describe error checking software utilities. (4)

   b Explain why error checking is necessary when a video clip is being streamed across the machines
      on a network. (3)

   (OCR AS Computing paper 2506 – Jun 2006)

3 When data is transferred from the main memory to the hard disk drive, parallel data transmission
   is used.

   (i)   State what is meant by parallel data transmission and give a reason why it would be used
         in this example. (2)

   (ii) During the process of transferring the data to the hard disk drive interrupts are used.
         Describe what an interrupt is and explain why it is necessary in this case. (4)

   (iii) Explain why half duplex data transmission is used in this example of data transfer. (2)

   (OCR AS Computing paper 2506 – Jun 2006)

4 a State two differences between a LAN and a WAN. (2)

   b When data is transmitted over a network it can be transmitted using either circuit switching or
      packet switching.
      Explain what is meant by circuit switching and by packet switching, giving an advantage of
      using each. (4)

   c Explain why communication interfaces are arranged in a layered fashion. (2)

   (OCR AS Computing paper 2506 – Jun 2006)

5 10110110   10101010   11010000   10001111

   The four bytes of data have been received after being transmitted from one piece of hardware to
   another. One of the four bytes has been rejected.

   a State which byte has been rejected, explaining why. (3)

   b Another four bytes are transmitted along with their checksum.
      Explain what is meant by a checksum. (2)
      Calculate the checksum for the four bytes given, showing your working:
      01001000   10000110   00010001   00010000

   (3)

   (OCR AS Computing paper 2506 – Jun 2006)

Chapter 6 Implications of Computer Use

The use of computer systems has changed in little more than three generations. From the home secretary stating to the House of Commons that there will only ever be a need for three computers in Britain to the present situation, where most of the population either have their own computer or have the use of one, and computers being a part of almost every aspect of modern life. Human beings are not designed to change so quickly, which has led to particular problems along with the undoubted advantages that have accompanied the march of computer technology through every aspect of society.

1. Economic implications

< Discuss >

Discuss the implications of the introduction of computer systems to an organisation, e.g. a school, a supermarket or a building supply company. Try, at the moment, to limit your thoughts to the economic implications and then expand as we go through the rest of this chapter.

Computers began to have an economic effect on society from the moment that they were made available to businesses. A bank now had a machine that could automatically keep records of customers' accounts and keep them up to date. It meant that the bank no longer had to employ clerks to work everything out by hand and keep hard copy records of every account. This, in turn, meant that the process became very much cheaper for the banks and this meant that they could bring down their costs (in the 1950s the standard charge made for a transaction of any type was half a crown!). In a time where a shop assistant was earning about £3 a week it was impossible for ordinary people to afford to have an account. Nowadays we expect that our banking will be free (if we stay in credit on our account) and most people have one or more accounts. Is this a good thing? Not to the bank clerks who were put out of a job. Think about the wider implications of this. People now had accounts, so bills like the gas bill could be paid by cheque (and then by direct debit, without any person being involved). Paying by cheque meant that the bill and the payment could be posted to head office and nobody had to go to the gas board office in town to pay in cash. This was a marvellous improvement for the customer, as it was so much more convenient, and wonderful for the gas board too because they could shut their offices and make some money on selling the buildings. But what about the people who worked there? What about the person with a query about the bill? They cannot go into the shop any more to have a chat with the people and try to sort out their problem. What about the cut in the number of people going into town because they no longer have to? What effect does this have on all sorts of things, from town centre shops who see a cut in numbers of people, to the bus services which lose passengers and start shutting down services? We could continue with this, but the point is that while the computer was well away from these effects its introduction had consequences for many parts of society that seem disconnected.

2. Social implications

It is very difficult to compartmentalise the effects that the introduction of computers can have, as we shall see now.

It used to be said that British society was divided on lines of class, which then changed to wealth. These two types of division probably still exist to a greater or lesser extent today, but there is a new type of division which is becoming far more important than anything else. It is the access to and the ability to use the new technologies. I am able to use the new technologies and they play a large part in my life. However, my neighbour does not have a computer and would find great difficulty in learning how to use one. If I want to book a holiday I decide where I want to go and then go on to the Internet and get the best deal that I can. My neighbour wants the same holiday but has to go into the travel agency to book it. This means that we have the same holiday but my neighbour pays more for it than I do. This comes on top of the fact that because of the computer equipment that I have I am able to work from home, saving money on travel and being able to plan my days flexibly rather than having to be in one place for the whole day. My neighbour has these extra costs and is tied to a rigid timetable for the day. I have developed an expertise with the computer systems that I use, which has increased my qualifications, and means that I am on a higher wage level than my neighbour, and in addition I have greater work protection because my company has lower costs. In this way the gap between the 'haves' and 'have-nots' of technology use is getting wider.

Social effects also impact on young people's lives. Children tend now to stay in as they have all they want on their computers.

3. Legal implications

There used to be simple laws about what could and could not be said about other people, what sort of information could be stored or even looked at, and the enforcement of these laws was fairly straightforward because everyone knew them and understood them. Now it is very much more difficult. Much more information is available to people, it is in a different form and the boundaries are not so obvious any more. If a business has some information stored on paper in a filing cabinet in their offices, and if I read that information without permission it is fairly obvious that this is illegal and what law is involved because I must have broken into the office and filing cabinet in order to read it. However, if I manage to bring the information up on my computer because it is in a computerised format, then what law have I broken?

Is it right for an organisation to store confidential information about me and pass it on to another business? Is it right for my

< Discuss >

Discuss whether it would be better for children to be playing football in the street or a football game on their computer. Is it right for children to have mobile phones? Think about the medical effects (thumbs used for texting, possible damage because of the signal strength, etc.) as well as the social and anti-social uses.

Discuss the social implications of the introduction of computers into the organisation that you discussed in Chapter 6.1.

doctor to allow information about me held on a computer system at the surgery to be passed on to others? What about passing it on to the hospital? What about to my employer? Would it make any difference if my employer wanted to know so that they could make arrangements to make my life easier and they could only do this if they knew about any medical problems I have?

What about if I have a personal website and I want to have music playing in the background?

What if I decide to download some pornography, which is illegal in this country but is legal in other parts of the world and consequently is available on the Internet?

< Discuss >

Discuss the legal implications that can arise because of the increase in computer use and information stored digitally.

Try to find out about the provisions of the Data Protection Act, the Computer Misuse Act and the copyright laws.

4. Ethical implications

If the people of this country have decided that certain types of pornography and drugs are illegal, then what right do people in other countries have to put information about them on the Internet, making it almost impossible for the authorities in this country to control it? What right do we in this country have to influence others throughout the world to our views on life? Look at many of the sites on the Internet and you will get the impression that the way of life in the developed West is the only right one and the culture to which we should all aspire.

If the supermarket offers lower prices then that is probably a good thing for most people, but what about the shopkeepers that it puts out of work and what about the old people who go to the local shops more for a social gathering rather than to buy food?

5. Environmental implications

If I can work from home I do not need to use my car to go to work, not only saving fuel resources but cutting pollution and meaning that the new bypass does not need to be built because there are fewer vehicles on the road. If I use the technology to hold a meeting by using teleconferencing with one of my customers rather than catching a plane to have a face-to-face meeting, then perhaps the number of flights will be cut and it will not be necessary to build that extra runway! If I buy my new television from a website the company I buy from does not need to have a shop, which means the goods do not need to be sent to a shop for me to look at them, thus saving the need to light and heat premises.

The paragraph above is deliberately one-sided. All the consequences have been positive ones and it is likely that, reading it, the impression is that the new technologies can only be a good thing. But temper those views with the sort of arguments put forward in the other parts of this chapter. Consider, also, other implications, such as the effects of all the toxic materials and

< Discuss >

Discuss whether longer and longer passwords actually add anything to a security measure. What about using passwords that are not words from a dictionary? Does it make any difference?

Is a user ID a privacy/ confidentiality measure? To answer this question think about what the ID tells the computer system and what the system can then do for that person. When is it not necessary to have an ID, though a password would still probably be a good idea?

What about if the data is more important than the sort of data we normally have on our systems?

heavy metals used in the manufacture of the hardware and our insistence on always having the most up-to-date of everything – is it really necessary to get another new mobile phone? Do businesses really need to change all their computer systems every two years?

6. Steps that can be taken to maintain confidentiality of data

Steps that we all take to protect our own work would include passwords of varying degrees of complexity.

Encryption is a method that can be used to protect the data

One way to stop other people seeing the data is to not let anyone use the computer. This is a bit extreme, but the idea is a good one. It can range from angling the screen so that nobody walking past the desk can see the screen to locking the computer room.

Large organisations that store people's personal data are controlled in what they can and cannot store by a law called the Data Protection Act. This lays down rules about what data can be stored and for how long. It also states that organisations must declare who within the organisation can be allowed to see personal data.

One of the problems with legislation is that policing it is almost impossible.

< Activity >

Find stories in the news about data that has been lost or has gone missing recently. Is it important?

< Discuss >

Discuss the difference between encryption and coding of data. Encryption is a method that can be used to protect the data. Do I really mean 'protect the data', or do I mean 'stop other people seeing the data'? What is the difference?

END OF CHAPTER QUESTIONS

1   Discuss the effects on society of working from home.   (8)
2   Customers of a supermarket are worried about their details being stored along with other data when they agree to become part of a customer loyalty scheme. Discuss the concerns of the customers and the means that the supermarket can use to allay those fears.   (8)

< Discuss >

What other measures should be included in legislation?

Chapter 7 Designing Solutions to Problems

In this unit, we discuss how computer programs are written to solve problems. A computer program is a set of instructions written to perform a specific task. It does not have to be running on a computer. Mobile phones, mp3 players, microwave ovens and missile launchers all operate using computer programs.

Although programs can be very different, they typically involve collecting some input data, processing this data in some way and outputting the result.

Figure 2.1 MP3 Player

Figure 2.2 Missile launcher

Figure 2.3 Typical operation of a computer program

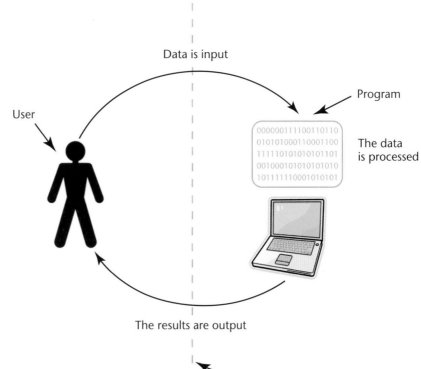

In this chapter, we will discuss the design of the different stages of a program, as shown in Figure 2.2:

■ Designing the user interface – how the data will be input and output
■ Designing the data that is used in the program
■ Designing the processing that needs to be done on the data.

We will also discuss how Rapid Application Development can be used as a design strategy.

1. Designing the user interface

The importance of good interface design

When designing a computer program, a lot of care needs to be taken to ensure that:

- the user can input the data easily
- the output is clear and understandable.

A program that achieves these aims is said to be **user-friendly**. A good design is a design that is user-friendly, not necessarily a design which looks good. A user-friendly interface should be **effective**, **efficient** and **satisfying** for the end user. These three characteristics support each other.

An effective user interface is one that allows the user to input and output all the data accurately. This will reduce errors made while operating the program, which could be costly for the user.

An efficient user interface is one that makes the best use of the facilities available to the program. These include processor time – the more efficient the user interface is, the quicker it will respond to any interaction from the user. It also includes making good use of any input or output devices or media available such as screen or paper space. An efficient user interface will increase the productivity of the program for the user.

A satisfying user interface is one that the end user is comfortable with and enjoys using. The program should be easy to learn. This can be achieved by using familiar tools, allowing the user to reapply their existing skills to the new program. The user can then focus on the task to be performed and not on learning how to use the program. This keeps down training costs and also improves morale.

< Example >

Good interface design can be a matter of life and death.

In 1983, during the cold war, Korean Airlines flight 007 from the USA to South Korea was shot down by the Soviet Union, killing all 269 passengers. Tensions flared between the USA and the Soviet Union and this could have led to nuclear war.

Reportedly, the accident was caused by poor user interface design. The input allowed the pilots to enter one digit incorrectly when setting the course for the autopilot. Furthermore, the output from the instruments did not allow the pilots to see easily that they were off-course. As a result, the plane flew into Soviet air space where it was interpreted as an American attack.

From: news.bbc.co.uk

Figure 2.4 Good interface design can be a matter of life and death

< Activity >

1 Earlier versions of the Windows operating system required the user to press the 'Start' button when they wanted to turn off their computer. Similarly, earlier versions of Mac OS required users to drag the icon for a CD-ROM to the trashcan in order to eject the disk.
From your own experience, or by doing some research, find as many other examples as you can of user interfaces which are counter-intuitive, confusing or can lead to errors.

2 Find and print a screenshot of an interactive website such as a forum or social networking site. Stick the screenshot onto a poster and annotate it showing elements that you consider to be of good design, and elements which you think need to be improved, giving reasons. Remember to focus on aspects of the design that make the website user-friendly.

Designing input screens

Very often, the user interface requires data to be input using a keyboard and mouse into an input screen. This will usually take the form of a Graphical User Interface (GUI) or a form-based interface as described in Chapter 2.4.

Here are some factors which should be considered when designing an input screen.

The User

It is important to remember who the user is while designing the input screen. For example, Figure 2.5 shows the user interface of a word processor for very young children. Notice how different it is from the word processor you normally use. Apart from age, you

Figure 2.5 Word processor for very young children

should also consider the level of computer literacy as well as any disabilities the user may have. This will allow you to select the most appropriate hardware and layouts for the range of users of the system.

Layout

It is important to take advantage of all the space available and make sure that the display is not cluttered. Grouping items together and using headings and subheadings can also make it easier for the users to find what they want.

Order

The user is likely to read the screen from left to right and from top to bottom. So, the title and most important information should come first. Action buttons for the end of the process (such as 'Next Screen' or 'Submit') should be near the bottom and to the right. Also, if the user interface is a form to be filled from a paper version, then the items on the screen should normally be in the same order as on the paper version.

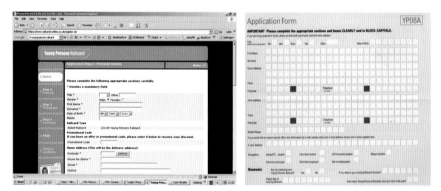

Figure 2.6 Electronic and paper-based form

Validation

The interface should, whenever possible, reject any data which are obviously wrong as they do not fit preset rules. Chapter 3.2 describes different validation checks that can be carried out.

GUI objects

When designing a graphical user interface (GUI), the objects available should be used to make the data input efficient and help avoid input errors. These include textboxes, drop-down lists, option buttons, check boxes, list boxes, command buttons, menus and toolbars. Textboxes should reflect the length of the input expected.

Online help and information

The interface should keep the user informed about what the system is doing. For example, if an input is rejected, the interface should explain why. If a process is likely to take a long time, a progress bar can be provided to indicate that the processing is being done and how long it will take. Any additional help should be easily available and relevant to what the user is currently doing wherever possible.

Designing data capture forms

A data capture form is a form that is used to collect data that will be input into a computer program.

If the data capture form is well designed, inputting the data on the form into the program will be easier. Therefore, the design of the data capture form is an important part of the design of the user interface.

Some factors that should be considered when designing a data capture form are given below.

Layout

The data fields and their layout on the data capture form should match the layout of the input form on the screen, with a one-to-one correspondence as far as possible. This will allow the user to easily switch between looking at the data capture form and the screen while inputting the data. This consistency of layout should be maintained within the elements of the screen. For example, if a drop-down list is to be used on screen, then the data capture form should have a vertical list of the same items, in the same order, from which the person filling the form can select one.

Instructions

If the form is filled in incorrectly, the data will most probably be unusable and cannot be input. Unlike an onscreen form, a data capture form cannot give you an error message if the data has been filled in incorrectly. This makes it very important that the form should have very clear instructions indicating how it should be filled.

Readability

If the data on the form cannot be read, then it cannot be input into the program. Instructions should encourage the person filling in the form to write clearly and in block capitals where this is practical. One way to encourage this, is to use provide boxes for data such as names and dates, such that each box needs to be filled in with one character. This is also useful for limiting the number of characters entered on the form to the maximum allowed by the program.

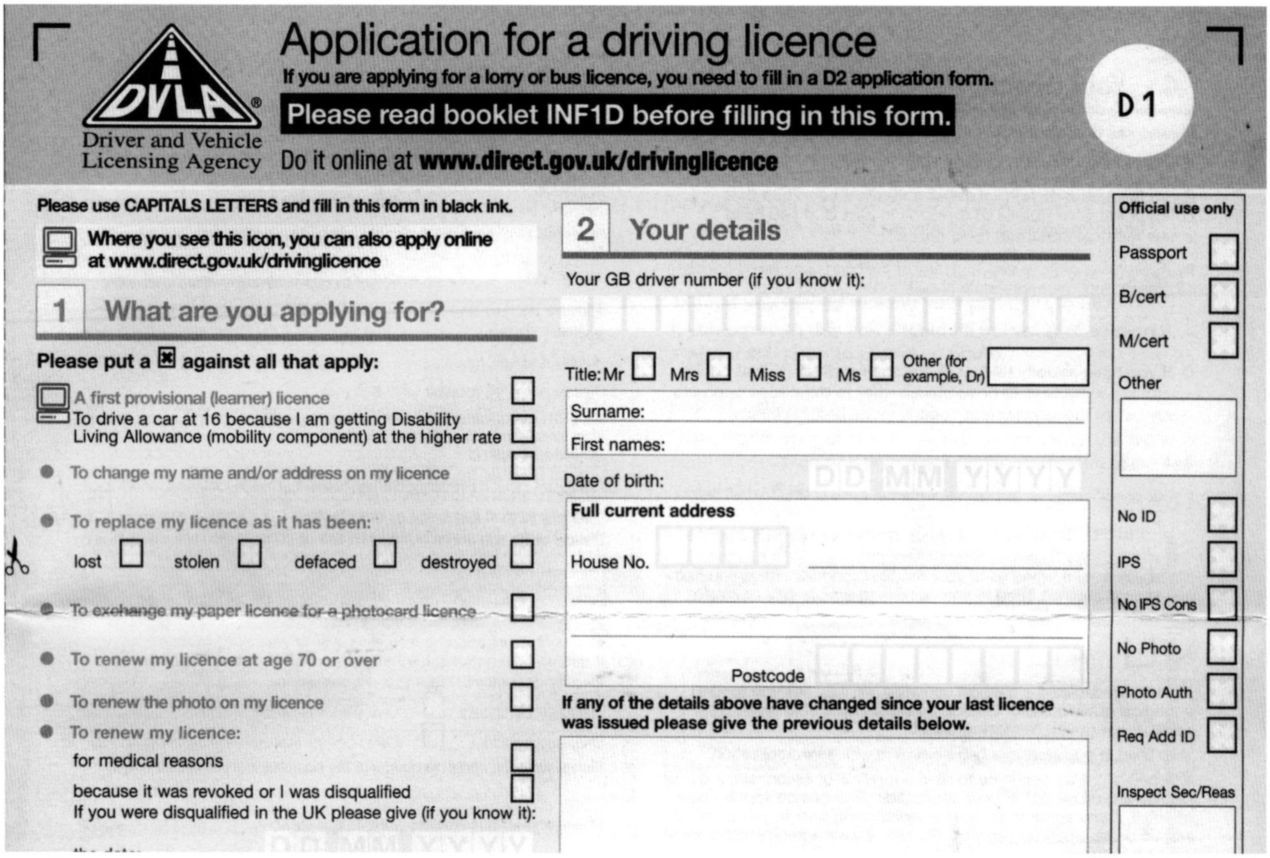

DVLA Driver and Vehicle Licensing Agency

Application for a driving licence

If you are applying for a lorry or bus licence, you need to fill in a D2 application form.

Please read booklet INF1D before filling in this form.

Do it online at www.direct.gov.uk/drivinglicence

D1

Please use CAPITALS LETTERS and fill in this form in black ink.

Where you see this icon, you can also apply online at www.direct.gov.uk/drivinglicence

1 What are you applying for?

Please put a ☒ against all that apply:

- A first provisional (learner) licence ☐
- To drive a car at 16 because I am getting Disability Living Allowance (mobility component) at the higher rate ☐
- To change my name and/or address on my licence ☐
- To replace my licence as it has been: lost ☐ stolen ☐ defaced ☐ destroyed ☐
- To exchange my paper licence for a photocard licence ☐
- To renew my licence at age 70 or over ☐
- To renew the photo on my licence ☐
- To renew my licence: for medical reasons ☐ because it was revoked or I was disqualified ☐

If you were disqualified in the UK please give (if you know it): the date: DD MM YYYY

2 Your details

Your GB driver number (if you know it):

Title: Mr ☐ Mrs ☐ Miss ☐ Ms ☐ Other (for example, Dr) ☐

Surname:

First names:

Date of birth: DD MM YYYY

Full current address

House No.

Postcode

If any of the details above have changed since your last licence was issued please give the previous details below.

Official use only: Passport ☐ B/cert ☐ M/cert ☐ Other ☐ No ID ☐ IPS ☐ No IPS Cons ☐ No Photo ☐ Photo Auth ☐ Req Add ID ☐ Inspect Sec/Reas ☐

Figure 2.7 Application form for a driving licence

< Activity >

Figure 2.7 shows part of the data capture form used to apply for a driving licence in the UK.

1 Suggest ways in which this data capture form could be improved.
2 Design a computer input screen that can be used to enter the information on the form into the computer.

Designing report layouts

A **report** is the presentation of the data from a computer program that has been selected, processed and presented to meet a specific need of the user, usually in printed form. A **report layout** describes which data should be output and in what position, often using tables and fields.

Just like an input screen, when designing a report layout you will need to consider the user and the hardware that will be used, as well as other factors such as what type and size of paper it will be printed on, or whether the report will be printed in colour.

You should always consider who is reading the report and what data they most need to see so that you can highlight the most relevant information. Often, graphical output, such as a pie chart, can be more effective than text for conveying the information.

Because a report can be printed and stored, it is more likely to be read out of context, at a later time or in a different place. It is therefore very important that the report contains a clear **title** which describes what the report contains.

You should remember that the report is a record of the result of processing the data at a specific time and that the same process may produce different results if the data changes. Therefore it is important for a report to show the **date** when it was printed, so that the reader can tell how current the information is.

Other types of interface

A good interface for a particular problem may not involve inputting data into a window on screen or producing printed reports.

A typical example is the use of touch screen interfaces, especially with menu-based systems. When designing a touch screen interface, you should ensure that contact areas are large enough to be used effectively. Most menu-based interfaces will also need an option to return to the previous menu or to start over.

You may have to make allowances in your design for people with disabilities and other special circumstances. For example, sound output can be used in addition to, or in place of, a visual output.

Finally, remember that programs do not necessarily run on a computer. **Embedded software** such as the software of a digital watch or a vending machine will also need to be designed before the program can be written. The user interface will typically include custom input methods such as buttons or other controls. The output may involve custom screens, LED lights or sound. Just remember to choose methods that will be most effective for the user and the task to be performed.

2. Determining the data requirements of a program

When designing a program, you also need to specify what data the program will need and how it will be stored. Designing the input and output requirements of the program should give you the majority of this data. However, it needs to be presented in a way that can easily be checked for completeness and referred to while the program is being written to avoid errors.

This can be done using a **data dictionary**. A data dictionary is a file which contains descriptions of, and other details about, the data in a program. These details include:

■ The identifier (name) for variables or fields which will be used to contain the data
■ The data type or data structure
■ The size of the data
■ Any validation that needs to be carried out on the data.

You will look at describing the data in a program in more detail in Chapter 9.

3. Modular design

As problems solved by computer programs have become bigger and more complex, it has become difficult for one person to devise a solution or to implement it on their own. A **modular, top-down design** can be used to tackle such problems.

In a top-down design, the task that the program needs to perform is split into smaller subtasks. These subtasks are then repeatedly split into even smaller subtasks. This is known as **stepwise refinement**. Eventually each task becomes so small that it can easily be programmed. The program for each subtask can then be implemented independently as a separate module, and then the modules can be put together to create a solution for the main problem.

For example, the software that controls a simple mobile phone would be very difficult to write, but it could be split into separate modules. Each module could represent one feature of the phone, such as making voice calls, sending text messages and the phone book. Each feature could then be split further. This can be shown in a **structure diagram** as in Figure 2.7.

Figure 2.8 Features of a mobile phone

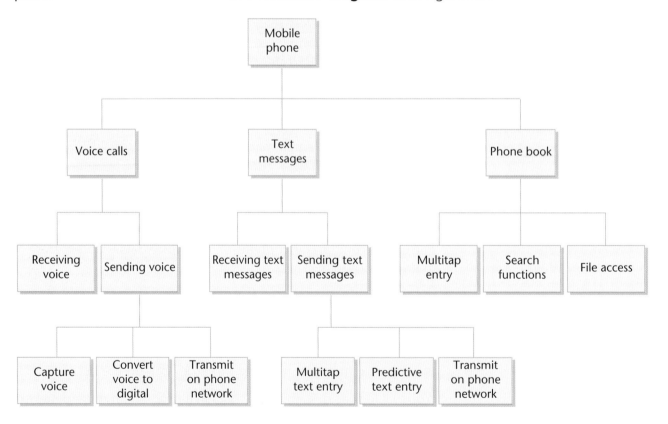

There are many advantages to using a top-down, modular design:

- The program is easier to write and test. Each module is small and can be written and tested independently.
- The design clearly shows how the different parts of the program relate to each other. This reduces errors caused by different parts of a large program interfering with each other.
- A team of programmers, each working on separate modules, can easily develop the program. The modules can be allocated according to the expertise of each programmer.
- The modules are written separately to perform a small, specific task, and they can be reused in other parts of the program or indeed in other programs whenever that task needs to be performed again. For example, in Figure 2.8, transmitting voice after it has been converted to digital data, or transmitting text message over the network is the same task and can be carried out by the same module.

Can you spot any other module in the structure diagram that can be reused?

< Activity >

A child minder wants to use a computer program to manage his or her business. In one part of the program, the child minder will keep a record of all the children that have been looked after, their enrolment when they apply, and the removal of their details when they leave. In another part of the program the child minder wants to keeps a record of each child's attendance on a daily basis. In a third part, the child minder should be able to calculate and send invoices to the parents of the children and keep track of the business's finances.

Produce a structure diagram to show a top-down design of the computer program. You should have at least three stages of stepwise refinement.

Figure 2.9 Computer programs can be used to manage all kinds of businesses

4. Designing algorithms

To design a solution to a problem, it is not enough to design what data is needed and how that data is going to be input and output. We need to design what the computer program will actually DO with the data that has been input in order to produce the output. This is called an **algorithm**.

A well-designed algorithm will list every instruction the computer needs to execute to solve the problem, and show the order in which these instructions should be executed.

Devising algorithms to solve problems is the essential skill which lies at the heart of this unit, and we shall revisit it in the other chapters, especially Chapters 8, 9 and 10. In this chapter, we are mainly concerned with how to write down the design of an algorithm.

Any description of the steps needed to solve a problem that can be understood and implemented by other programmers is a successful design. This could range from a piece of text in prose explaining the steps, to actual code in a programming language. However, an effective design will need to be somewhere in between these two extremes. It should be more structured than prose so that it can be easily followed, but less rigid than code so that you can concentrate on the logic in solving the problem instead of the rules of the particular language you are using.

We will look at two conventions that achieve this middle ground, namely **program flowcharts** and **pseudo-code**.

Program flowcharts

A program flowchart uses a diagram to show the operation of the algorithm. It uses a small number of conventional symbols to represent individual steps of the algorithm. Flow lines to show the order in which the steps are carried out connect these symbols. Some of the symbols that can be used are described in the table opposite.

> **Definition:** An algorithm is a sequence of steps designed to perform a particular task.

Start/Stop symbol 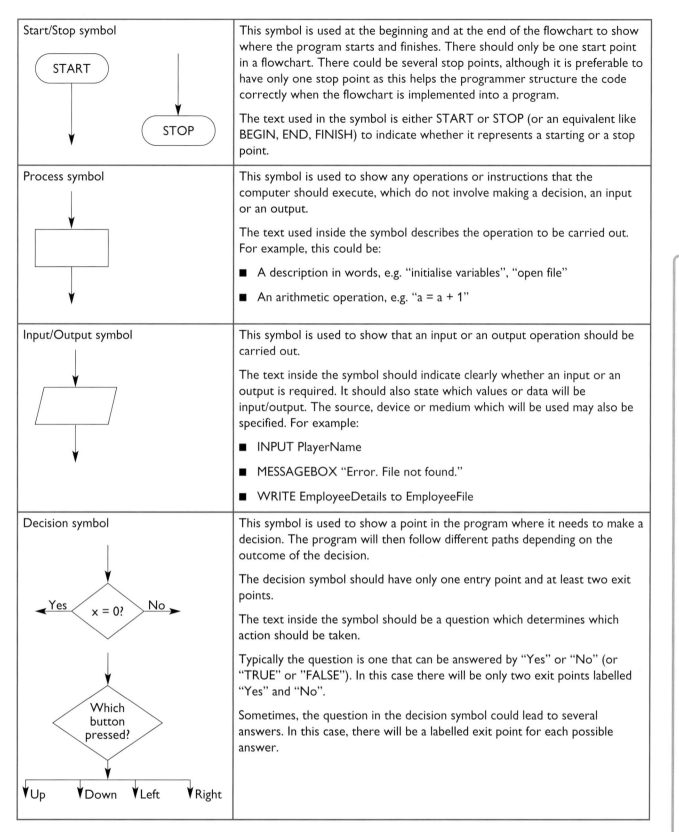	This symbol is used at the beginning and at the end of the flowchart to show where the program starts and finishes. There should only be one start point in a flowchart. There could be several stop points, although it is preferable to have only one stop point as this helps the programmer structure the code correctly when the flowchart is implemented into a program. The text used in the symbol is either START or STOP (or an equivalent like BEGIN, END, FINISH) to indicate whether it represents a starting or a stop point.
Process symbol	This symbol is used to show any operations or instructions that the computer should execute, which do not involve making a decision, an input or an output. The text used inside the symbol describes the operation to be carried out. For example, this could be: ■ A description in words, e.g. "initialise variables", "open file" ■ An arithmetic operation, e.g. "a = a + 1"
Input/Output symbol	This symbol is used to show that an input or an output operation should be carried out. The text inside the symbol should indicate clearly whether an input or an output is required. It should also state which values or data will be input/output. The source, device or medium which will be used may also be specified. For example: ■ INPUT PlayerName ■ MESSAGEBOX "Error. File not found." ■ WRITE EmployeeDetails to EmployeeFile
Decision symbol	This symbol is used to show a point in the program where it needs to make a decision. The program will then follow different paths depending on the outcome of the decision. The decision symbol should have only one entry point and at least two exit points. The text inside the symbol should be a question which determines which action should be taken. Typically the question is one that can be answered by "Yes" or "No" (or "TRUE" or "FALSE"). In this case there will be only two exit points labelled "Yes" and "No". Sometimes, the question in the decision symbol could lead to several answers. In this case, there will be a labelled exit point for each possible answer.

Subroutine symbol 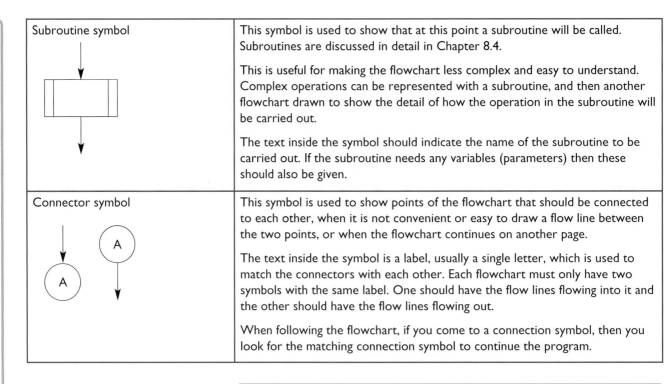	This symbol is used to show that at this point a subroutine will be called. Subroutines are discussed in detail in Chapter 8.4. This is useful for making the flowchart less complex and easy to understand. Complex operations can be represented with a subroutine, and then another flowchart drawn to show the detail of how the operation in the subroutine will be carried out. The text inside the symbol should indicate the name of the subroutine to be carried out. If the subroutine needs any variables (parameters) then these should also be given.
Connector symbol	This symbol is used to show points of the flowchart that should be connected to each other, when it is not convenient or easy to draw a flow line between the two points, or when the flowchart continues on another page. The text inside the symbol is a label, usually a single letter, which is used to match the connectors with each other. Each flowchart must only have two symbols with the same label. One should have the flow lines flowing into it and the other should have the flow lines flowing out. When following the flowchart, if you come to a connection symbol, then you look for the matching connection symbol to continue the program.

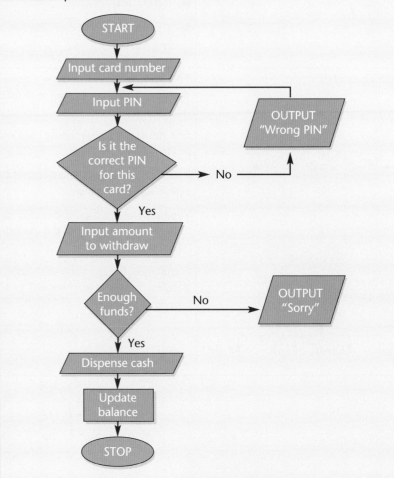

< Example >

The following flowchart describes an algorithm which a cash point can use to process cash withdrawal transactions.

Figure 2.10

Pseudo-code

Pseudo-code is an alternative method of describing an algorithm that uses text instead of a diagram.

Pseudo-code can be thought of as a simplified form of programming code. The prefix 'pseudo' usually means 'false' or 'not genuine'. It is used here because pseudo-code does not follow the strict rules of a programming language. However, it does use some of the keywords and layout techniques of programming languages to make the structure of the algorithm clear. Common programming language functions are mixed with English phrases to describe the individual steps of the algorithm.

For example, the algorithm for the cash point flowchart (Figure 2.10) can be written in pseudo-code as follows:

```
BEGIN
  INPUT CardNumber
  REPEAT
    INPUT PIN
    IF PIN is wrong for this CardNumber THEN
      OUTPUT "Wrong PIN"
    END IF
  UNTIL PIN is correct
  INPUT Amount
  IF there are enough funds THEN
    Dispense Cash
    Update customer's balance
  ELSE
    OUTPUT "Sorry, insufficient funds"
  END IF
END
```

By definition, there are no hard and fast rules for writing pseudo-code, but certain guidelines will ensure that the algorithm is clear:

■ Describe each step of the algorithm as briefly as possible.
■ Use uppercase letters with keywords and other parts of the pseudo-code which are closer to a programming language.
■ Use lowercase letters with parts of the pseudo-code which are closer to English.
■ If you use keywords to show the beginning and end of a block of code, then the code inside this block should be indented. You will read more about indentation in Chapter 11.3.

In this chapter, it is sufficient to focus on the general principles of pseudo-code and how it is written. The remaining chapters of this unit use pseudo-code to illustrate programming concepts. Learning these concepts will enable you to write effective pseudo-code that can easily be implemented in the programming language of your choice.

5. Rapid Application Development (RAD)

Rapid Application Development is a methodology for designing and writing software that includes producing successive prototype versions of the software until the final version is produced.

In Chapter 2.1 you studied different models of the systems development life cycle, including the waterfall and spiral models. The waterfall model ensures that a working version of the system is produced at the end of one cycle and therefore the system has to be fully designed, developed and tested at each stage of the cycle. In contrast, RAD is more similar to the spiral model – several increasingly refined prototypes are produced until you produce the final working version.

The typical operation of RAD is shown in Figure 2.11:

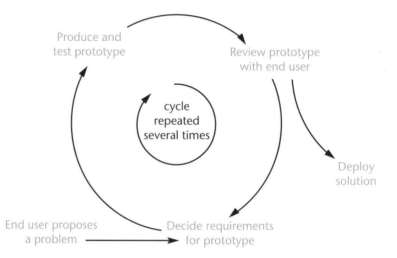

Figure 2.11

In order to solve the problem, the programmers produce a prototype with reduced functionality. This is then reviewed with the end user who can suggest changes which need to be made or key features which should be included in the next prototype. From this review, an improved prototype is created. This cycle is repeated several times producing successive prototypes, each one improving on the previous, until the final product is deployed. This is referred to as **iterative development**. Each cycle lasts typically one to three weeks.

Advantages of RAD include:

■ The end user is involved in the development process. This allows the development to be flexible and allow for changes in the user's requirements and prevents problems caused by the requirements not having been correctly understood in the first place.

- Using prototypes means that a tangible product can be seen earlier in the project. Even if the prototype has reduced functionality, it is much less abstract than the design, and so the end user has more confidence that the correct solution will be produced.
- Overall, the length of the development is usually shorter, compared to software developed using the waterfall model. This is because RAD uses a range of tools to help build prototypes quickly. These are called Computer Aided Software Engineering (CASE) tools.

Disadvantages of RAD include:

- It is not efficient when dealing with very large-scale projects. The initial prototypes are likely to be so different from the final product that a lot of rethinking of earlier prototypes becomes necessary.
- It focuses on the end result rather than on the processing and can produce solutions that are inefficient in the way they use available resources. This is partly due to the fact that RAD relies on tools which produce a prototype quickly.

< Example >

The basic principles behind RAD have been developed into a range of methodologies called Agile Development. An increasingly popular form of Agile Development is eXtreme Programming (XP), which advocates certain key practices such as pair programming (code is always written by two people working together) and an onsite customer (the end user should also always be available to answer questions that arise during the programming.)

Figure 2.12 Pair programming

END OF CHAPTER QUESTIONS

1　A school is organising an activities day for its Year 9 pupils. The activities offered are Sports, Craft, Performance or Discovery. Pupils register on a website indicating which activities they prefer.

Design an input screen for the website, where the pupils can enter their Name, Tutor group, and their first, second and third choice of activity. (8)

2　A bookshop produces a weekly report of the five most popular titles for fiction and non-fiction. This report is printed in colour on a large poster that is displayed around the bookshop.

Design a report layout for this report. (6)

3　A personal video recorder (PVR) has a hand-held remote controller with a small screen that can display four lines of 20 characters.

The controller displays a simple electronic programme guide of television programmes for the next seven days. The user can browse through the programme guide on the screen, one programme at a time.

The following information can be seen about each programme:

- the television channel
- the date
- the start time
- the finish time
- the title (which may be longer than 20 characters).

a Using the grid below design a layout for this information. You should indicate where each item will be displayed and you may annotate the diagram to explain how the interface will operate.

(6)

b As well as the display, the remote controller has buttons labelled UP, DOWN, LEFT, RIGHT, SELECT and EXIT.

Describe how the controller can be used to browse through the programme guide, select a TV programme and set it to be recorded on the PVR.

The quality of your written communication will be assessed in this answer. (6)

4   The amount of child benefit a family is entitled to depends on the number of eligible children being raised by the family. In 2008, it was £18.10 per week for the eldest child and £12.10 for every other child. (In other words, the family receive an extra £6 for the eldest child).

The following algorithm was written to input the number of children in a family and output their weekly child benefit entitlement.

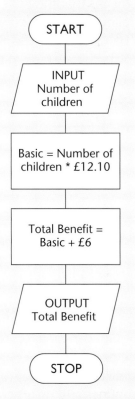

a Using the flowchart, state the value of the output if the input is:
   (i)   4
   (ii) 0   (2)
b Explain why the algorithm in the flowchart does not correctly solve the problem of calculating the child benefit entitlement.   (2)
c Design, using a flowchart, an algorithm to calculate the child benefit entitlement correctly.   (5)
5   Rapid Application Development (RAD) is to be used in the development of the software for controlling voting.
a Explain how the use of RAD can speed up the development process.   (2)
b Explain how the end user is involved during the testing and refining of the software.   (2)
c Describe **two** advantages, for the user, of using a RAD approach.   (4)

[OCR AS Computing paper 2506 – June 2006]

Chapter 8 The Structure of Procedural Programs

In this chapter, we discuss how to solve problems by writing algorithms in a procedural language. This means that the code contains instructions for the computer to follow. The simplest way to do this is to give a list of instructions to be carried out one after the other. For example, a program to calculate the average of two numbers would simply be:

```
INPUT number A
INPUT number B
LET Total = A + B
LET Average = Total / 2
OUTPUT Average
```

Obviously, all programs cannot be written as simply as this, or they would be very limited. For averages, different programs would have to be written to find the average of three, four or five numbers.

In this chapter, we discuss how code can be organised to control the flow of execution so that the same program can be executed in various ways other than starting from the beginning and continuing in sequence until the end. This includes control structures within the code, the use of subroutines and recursion.

1. Important definitions

Here are some terms that are used to describe the structure of programs. They will be explained in greater detail in the rest of this chapter. They are given here so that you have a single point to refer to if you need any of the definitions.

Statement: *a statement is a single instruction or step within a program.* Usually, each statement is written in one line of code. However, we shall see later in this chapter that this is not always the case.

Subroutine: *a subroutine is a set of instructions that perform a specific task as part of a larger program.* The main program will contain instructions to *call* the subroutine. When the subroutine is called, the program will transfer control to the subroutine and the instructions in the subroutine are executed, then control is transferred back to the main program.

Procedure: *a procedure is a subroutine that simply executes its statements and returns control to the main program.* It is usually called as an instruction to the computer.

Function: *a function is a subroutine that executes its statements and returns a single value.* It is usually called as part of an expression and the value returned can replace the function call in the expression.

Parameter: *a parameter is an item of data that is given to a procedure or function.* It is usually written in brackets after the name of the procedure or function.

Sequence: *a sequence is a control structure in which a set of instructions is each executed once, in the order in which they are written.*

Selection: *selection is a control structure in which an option of statements is provided and a condition is used to decide which (if any) statements should be executed.*

Iteration: *iteration is a control structure in which a group of statements is executed repeatedly.* It is also called a **loop** or **repetition**.

2. The three basic constructs

The three basic programming constructs: sequence, selection and iteration, allow us to control how the program will execute the statements in it.

Sequence

At the start of this chapter we saw the following program that calculates the average of two numbers:

```
BEGIN
  INPUT number A
  INPUT number B
  LET Total = A + B
  LET Average = Total / 2
  OUTPUT Average
END
```

This is an example of a **sequence**. To execute this program, the computer needs to start at the beginning, execute each statement once until it gets to the end and stops.

Selection

Selection allows us to select the statements which will be executed depending on a condition. How this is achieved varies in different languages but usually involve a variation of the *IF* statement and the *CASE* statement.

IF statements

A common format for an IF statement is given below. Items in the angled brackets need to be replaced as needed by the program. The ... indicates that there may be more than one instruction.

```
IF <condition> THEN
    <instructions to be executed>
    ...
END IF
```

A condition is an expression that has a value of TRUE or FALSE. If the condition is true then the instructions are executed.

Sometimes, the IF statement also contains instructions to be carried out if the condition is false.

```
IF <condition> THEN
    <instructions to be executed if the condition is true>
    ...
ELSE
    <instructions to be executed if the condition is false>
    ...
END IF
```

For example, here is part of an algorithm for logging onto a computer:

```
IF PasswordIsCorrect THEN
    Remove logon screen
    Open desktop
ELSE
    OUTPUT "Incorrect password. Please try again."
    Clear Username and Password entry field.
END IF
```

In this example, PasswordIsCorrect is the condition. When the program is implemented its value can be either TRUE or FALSE.

CASE statements

Another type of selection construct is the CASE statement. A CASE statement uses a variable instead of a condition to determine which instructions will be executed:

```
SELECT CASE <variable> OF
  CASE <value1>:
      <instructions to run if the variable has this value>
  CASE <value2>:
    <instructions to run if the variable has this value>
  CASE <value3>:
    <instructions to run if the variable has this value>
  ...
END SELECT
```

A CASE statement can be a very useful replacement for a series of IF statements whose conditions depend on the same variable. For example the code for a platform game will make the character move in different ways depending on which joypad button has been pressed. In this case, the variable which determines the code to be executed is the code for the button which has been pressed.

Figure 2.13 Super Mario Brothers game by Nintendo

```
SELECT CASE button
  CASE LeftButton
    Move character 1 step backwards
  CASE RightButton
    Move character 1 step forward
  CASE UpButton
    Make character jump
  CASE DownButton
    Make character duck
END SELECT
```

Iteration

Iteration allows a group of statements in the code to be executed several times. This is useful because we would otherwise have to write the instructions out the correct number of times.

Condition-controlled loops

We may not know, at the time of writing the code, how many times we want the instructions to be repeated. We instead have a condition which determines whether or not the instructions need to be executed. This is called a condition-controlled loop.

One kind of condition-controlled loop is the **WHILE** loop:

```
WHILE <condition>
   <instructions to be repeated>
   ...
END WHILE
```

When this code is executed, the condition is tested first. If this condition is true, then the instructions in the loop are executed. The computer then goes back to the beginning of the loop and tests the condition again. If the condition is still true, then the instructions in the loop are executed again. This is repeated as long as every time the condition is tested, it is true. However, if the condition is false, then the loop ends, and control transfers to the next line after the loop (i.e. after END WHILE).

Note that if the condition is false the first time the loop is executed, then the loop ends immediately and the instructions in the loop are not executed.

Another kind of condition-controlled loop is the **REPEAT UNTIL** loop:

```
REPEAT
   <instructions to be repeated>
   ...
UNTIL <condition>
```

In this loop the instructions are executed first. When the computer reaches the end (UNTIL <condition>) the condition is tested. If the condition is false, then the computer executes the instructions inside the loop again. This is repeated after each cycle as long as the condition is false. However, if the condition is true, then the loop ends and control transfers to the next line.

Notice some of the differences between the WHILE loop and the REPEAT UNTIL loop.

WHILE	REPEAT UNTIL
Condition is tested *before* each cycle	Condition is tested *after* each cycle
Repeats if the condition is TRUE and exits if the condition is FALSE	Repeats if the condition is FALSE and exits if the condition is TRUE
The instructions in the loop may never be executed (if the condition is FALSE at the beginning)	The instructions in the loop will always be executed at least once

By changing the conditions and/or some of the data in the program, it is possible to convert a WHILE loop into a REPEAT UNTIL loop that performs the same function. For example, the following loops both output the numbers 1 to 5:

```
Set i to 0
WHILE i < 5
  Add 1 to i
  OUTPUT i
END WHILE
```
```
Set i to 1
REPEAT
  OUTPUT i
  Add 1 to i
UNTIL i = 5
```

Some languages have different variations on these basic condition-controlled loops.

Regardless of which condition-controlled loop you use, you need to carefully make sure that the loop will end. If the condition in a while loop can never be FALSE then the loop will just repeat forever. This is called an **infinite loop** and is usually caused by an error in the logic of your algorithm. A similar situation will occur if the condition in a REPEAT UNTIL loop can never be TRUE.

For example, if we omit the instruction "Add 1 to i" in the above algorithms we get:

```
Set i to 0
WHILE i < 5
  OUTPUT i
END WHILE
```
```
Set i to 1
REPEAT
  OUTPUT i
UNTIL i = 5
```

In the WHILE loop the value of i will always be 0 and this is less than 5. The condition to stop the loop will never be met and it will loop endlessly, printing 0 each time. The REPEAT UNTIL loop will also loop endlessly as the value of i will always be 1.

Count-controlled loops

A different type of loop is a count-controlled loop. This is often called a **FOR** loop:

```
FOR <variable> = <starting value> TO <end value>
   <instructions to be executed>
...
NEXT
```

A FOR loop uses a variable to determine whether the instructions should be repeated. This variable is given starting and end values. The first time the loop is executed, the variable takes the starting value. When the computer gets to the end of the loop (NEXT), the value of the variable is typically incremented to the next value and the instructions are repeated. This continues until the variable reaches the end value. The instructions are then executed one more time (with the end value).

This can be explained using the following example:

```
01   FOR i = 1 TO 5
02     OUTPUT i*i
03   NEXT
```

Line 01 tells us that the control variable is *i* and it will have a starting value of 1 and an end value of 5. When the computer executes line 01, it will set the value of i to 1 (the starting value). The instructions in the loop (line 02) then get executed so the computer will output 1*1 which is 1. When it gets to line 03, the variable is incremented to the next value so *i* becomes 2 and the instructions in the loop (line 02) are executed again. This time the computer outputs 2*2 which is 4. This is repeated until i becomes the end value of 5. This will be the last iteration, so line 02 is executed for the last time outputting 5*5 which is 25.

Note that every FOR loop can be rewritten as a WHILE loop or a REPEAT UNTIL loop. You will need to add code which initialises the control variable (gives it a starting value) and which increments the starting value. The following code performs the same function as the example of the FOR loop just given:

```
01   LET i = 1          01   LET i = 1
02   WHILE i <= 5       02   REPEAT
03     OUTPUT i * i     03     OUTPUT i * i
04     i = i + 1        04     i = i + 1
05   END WHILE          05   UNTIL i > 5
```

3. Nesting constructs

Sometimes, the instructions inside a construct like an IF statement or a loop contain other constructs. This is called **nesting** a construct inside another.

Nesting constructs gives programmers the flexibility to write complex and powerful algorithms. However, care needs to be taken to ensure that the constructs are correctly nested. Each construct needs to be 'completely' within the instructions of another. The beginnings and ends of the constructs cannot overlap. Indenting the instructions in the constructs is one good way of ensuring this. The importance of using the correct indentation is explained fully in Chapter 11.3.

Here is an improved algorithm for logging onto a computer that we saw in Chapter 7.2:

```
01    Initialise NumberOfTries to 0
02    WHILE NumberOfTries < 3 and correct password not entered
03      Add 1 to NumberOfTries
04      Input Password
05      IF Password is correct THEN
06        Open desktop
07      ELSE
08        OUTPUT "Incorrect password. Please try again."
09      END IF
10    END WHILE
11    IF NumberOfTries = 3 and correct password not entered THEN
12      OUTPUT "Your account has been blocked"
13    END IF
```

Note how lines 03–09 are an IF statement that is nested inside the WHILE loop (02 to 10).

If two or more FOR loops are nested in each other, sometimes the control variable is stated on the NEXT line, to remind you to which FOR line it refers. For example, the code for filling in a 10 by 10 table with the numbers 1 to 100 may look like this:

```
01 FOR Row = 1 TO 10
02   FOR Column = 1 TO 10
03     Calculate value of ((Row - 1) * 10) + Column
04     Enter this value in table at position Row, Column
05   NEXT Column
04 NEXT Row
```

When this code is implemented and line 01 is executed, Row will be set to 1 at line 01, and Column will be set to 1 at line 02. The inner FOR loop, lines 03 to 05 will then be executed until Column = 10.

Only when the inner FOR loop has completed a full set of iterations can the control then pass to line 06 so that Row becomes 2. The outer loop then goes into its second iteration so lines 02 to 06 need to be executed again (which involves 10 new iterations of the inner loop). If you attempt to swap lines 05 and 06, this will generate an error as the program will need to end a loop while another loop, which is nested in it, has not ended. Notice how indentation has been used in the algorithm to make this structure clearer.

4. Subroutines

When a **subroutine** is defined it is given an identifier and some instructions to be executed. The identifier is the name of the subroutine. It is used to call the subroutine. 'To call the subroutine' means to request that the instructions in the subroutine be executed.

Two types of subroutines are **procedures** and **functions**. We discuss the differences between them later.

A procedure can be defined using the following format:

```
PROCEDURE <identifier(name) of the procedure>
  <instructions to be executed>
  ...
END PROCEDURE
```

In the main program, there should be a line that calls this procedure. This line will use the identifier of the procedure as an instruction (just like the other instructions built into the language). When this line is executed the execution of the main program pauses while control is passed to the subroutine. When the subprogram finishes, control goes back to the main program and it carries on from where it left off.

Parameters

Sometimes a procedure needs some data to carry out its instructions. This data needs to be specified when the procedure is defined. This is usually done by adding some variables, typically in brackets, after the identifier, as shown below. These variables are called the **parameters** of the procedure:

```
PROCEDURE <identifier of the procedure> (<parameters>)
  <instructions to be executed>
  ...
END PROCEDURE
```

When the procedure is called the actual values of these variables need to be supplied. These actual values are also called

arguments. The instructions in the procedure are then executed using the actual values substituting the parameters in the instructions. This is referred to as 'passing parameters' to the procedure. How parameters are passed to procedures will be discussed in more detail in Unit 3 Chapter 19.1.

It is often necessary to declare the data types of the parameters when you define the procedure. Take for example:

```
PROCEDURE PrintDetails (Name:String, Copies:Integer)
  Load details of Name from File
  Print the details loaded Copies times.
END PROCEDURE
```

In this example the name of the procedure is PrintDetails. The procedure has two parameters:

- Name – which is of data type String
- Copies – which is of data type Integer.

We discuss data types in fuller detail in Chapter 9.1.

When this procedure is called, actual values will be given for Name and Copies. For example:

PrintDetails("Jean Smith",4)

In this case, when the algorithm for PrintDetails is being executed, Name will be set to "Jean Smith" and Copies will be set to 4. This will cause the procedure to print four copies of Jean Smith's details.

Functions

A **function** is a subroutine similar to a procedure and it is defined with an identifier and some instructions to be executed and may also have parameters.

```
FUNCTION <identifier> (<parameters if any>)
  <instructions to be executed>
  ...
END FUNCTION
```

The significant difference is that a function returns a single value to the main program that called it.

The instructions in a function will need to include an instruction to set the return value. This is usually done using the name of the function as a variable in the definition, or by using a special keyword such as RETURN. For example, here are two versions of a function that returns the higher of its two parameters:

```
01   FUNCTION                    01  FUNCTION
     Higher(a,b)                     Higher(a,b)
02    IF a > b THEN             02   IF a > b THEN
03     Higher = a               03     RETURN a
04    ELSE                      04   ELSE
05     Higher = b               05     RETURN b
06    END IF                    06   END IF
07   END FUNCTION               07  END FUNCTION
```

The main program that calls the function needs to be told what to do with the value returned by the function. As a result, a function is usually used within an expression in the main program and not as an instruction on its own. The call to the function is used like a variable in the main program – the instructions in the function are executed, and the return value replaces the function call in the main program.

It is often necessary to declare the data type of the return value when you define the function:

```
FUNCTION Interest (Amt:Currency, Rate:Real, Yrs:Integer): Currency
   ...
END FUNCTION
```

This tells us that:

■ the name of the function is Interest
■ the function has three parameters, which are:
  ▪ Amt – of data type Currency
  ▪ Rate – of data type Real
  ▪ Yrs – of data type Integer.

The return value of the function is of data type Currency.

Recursion

Recursion is when a subroutine (a procedure or a function) calls itself.

The recursive subroutine is executed as normal until it gets to the line where it calls itself. At this point the subroutine is paused and a new call to the same subroutine is started.

If a new subroutine is started every time the subroutine is called the process would go on indefinitely (or until the computer does not have enough resources to cope with the number of suspended subroutines). Therefore, a recursive subroutine usually has parameters, and there is a case where, based on the value of these parameters, the subroutine can be executed and exit without needing to call itself. This is known as the **stopping condition**.

Once the stopping condition has been reached, the subroutine is executed completely and then control is passed back to the previous call that can now be executed to completion. This continues until the original call has been executed.

Here is the outline of a typical recursive procedure:

```
Procedure <name of the procedure> (<parameters>)
IF <stopping condition> THEN
    <Instructions to be executed for the stopping condition these
    ... instructions do not include a call to the subroutine>
ELSE
    <Instructions for all other cases these instructions will call the
    ... subroutine again usually with different parameters which will
    ... take the process closer to the stopping condition.>
END IF
```

Let's consider the following function:

```
01 FUNCTION Factorial (integer n) : integer
02   IF n = 1 THEN
03     RETURN 1
04   ELSE
05     RETURN n * Factorial(n - 1)
06   END IF
07 END FACTORIAL
```

The procedure is recursive because it calls itself in line 05. The stopping condition occurs when n = 1. In this case line 03 gets executed and the procedure can terminate without needing to call itself.

Let's consider what happens if the main program contains the instruction:

```
OUTPUT Factorial(2)
```

We shall trace the execution of this recursive call. This means we shall follow the execution step by step, noting which lines are executed, what happens when each line is executed and where recursive calls are made.

For a recursive algorithm, this is best done in a diagram, as illustrated in Figure 2.14.

The output instruction cannot be executed until the value of Factorial(2) has been returned. So the function Factorial is called with n set to 2. When the IF statement in line 02 is executed, n is

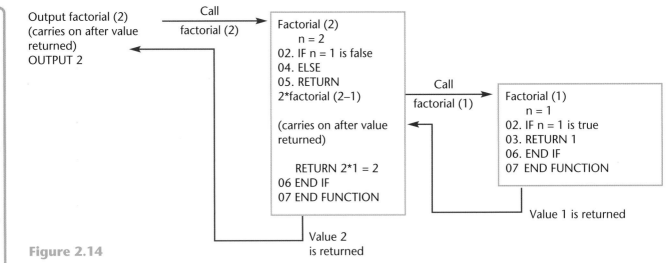

Figure 2.14

not equal to 1, so control goes to the ELSE part and to line 05. Line 05 cannot be executed because it contains the recursive call Factorial(n-1). In this case, n-1 is 2. The execution of the Factorial(2) is therefore paused on line 05, until Factorial(1) has been evaluated.

A new function call is made to Factorial(1). In this call the value of n is set to 1. In line 02, the IF statement will be TRUE, so line 03 is executed, which sets the return value to 1. The call to Factorial(1) then runs to completion and the value 1 is returned to the preceding call.

The preceding call can now continue from line 05 as the value of Factorial(1) has been returned. In this call the value of n is 2. So here, line 05 sets the return value to 2 * 1, which is 2. This call also runs to completion and the value 2 is returned to the main program. The main program can now output the value returned for Factorial(2), which is 2.

Note that if the original call had a higher value of n, say Factorial(8), then there would be several successive calls (each with a value of n, which is 1 less than the preceding call) until the stopping condition is met.

Every recursive algorithm can be written as an iterative algorithm. For example, here is an iterative version of the algorithm for the function Factorial:

```
01  FUNCTION Factorial (Integer n): Integer
02    current_number = n
03    answer_so_far = 1
04    WHILE current_number > 1
05      answer_so_far = answer_so_far * current_number
06      current = current_number - 1
07    LOOP
08    RETURN answer_so_far
09  END Factorial
```

The following table compares the iterative algorithm to the recursive version of the same algorithm:

Iteration	Recursion
Uses a loop to repeat instructions. There is an end condition to the loop that decides when to stop looping. The loop must include instructions that move a tracking variable towards the end condition.	Repeats by calling itself with simplified (smaller) arguments. There is a stopping condition that causes the subroutine to terminate without calling itself. The simplified arguments used in the recursion must eventually lead to the stopping condition.
There is only one function call – so one set of variables. This means that executing the iterative algorithm will use less memory.	There are many function calls, each with its own set of variables that are distinct from the variables of the other function calls. This means that it will take more memory during execution.
You need variables to keep track, e.g. a counter for the loop. These variables usually need to be initialised before the loops start. Because of the need to keep track of the variables as the loop progresses, the code can be more difficult to write or understand.	A new set of variables is automatically created on each function call. The code is also usually simpler to understand and closer to the way a human would explain the algorithm.

END OF CHAPTER QUESTIONS

1   Explain what is meant by:
    (a) Sequence
    (b) Selection
    (c) Iteration. (6)

2   (a) State **three** different types of iteration construct. In each case state how its use differs from the other two. (6)

(b) Consider the following algorithm in pseudo-code:

```
INPUT A,B
OUTPUT A,B
IF B = 0 THEN
    C = A
ELSE
    C = A DIV B
END IF
OUTPUT C
```

Write down the outputs produced by the algorithm if:

(i) A = 8, B = 2

(ii) A = 6, B = 0.   (4)

[OCR AS Computing paper 2506 – June 2006]

3   Consider the following algorithms, called Module 1 and Module 2:

```
MODULE 1                          MODULE 2
INPUT X                           INPUT X
WHILE X IS NOT 1 DO               REPEAT
A=5                               A=5
IF X=2 THEN                       IF X=2 THEN
   X=3                               X=3
ELSE                              ELSE
   X=1                               X=1
ENDIF                             ENDIF
OUTPUT A AND X                    OUTPUT A AND X
ENDWHILE                          UNTIL X=1
OUTPUT X                          OUTPUT X
```

(a) Write down the outputs from each of the Modules above, if the initial value of X is 1.   (4)

(b) Explain the difference between a WHILE…ENDWHILE loop and a REPEAT…UNTIL loop.   (2)

[OCR AS Computing paper 2506 – June 2006]

4   **(a)** State what is meant by a:

(i) procedure   (1)

(ii) function.   (1)

(b) Consider the following algorithm:

```
01  Function Test (x)
02     IF x = 1 THEN
03       Test = 1
04     ELSE
05       Test = x + Text(x - 1)
06     END IF
07  END TEST
```

(i) State the output from this algorithm when the initial value of X is 5.   (1)

(ii) Identify, from the algorithm, reasons why this is an example of recursion.   (2)

[OCR AS Computing paper 2506 – January 2007]

Chapter 9 Data Types and Data Structures

In this chapter we discuss the data that is used in most programming languages to solve problems. We consider different types of data, such as numbers and text in detail, how to select the correct type for a given problem, and how that affects the amount of storage the program will need.

We also discuss how individual items of data can be organised into data structures and files.

1. Data types

A **data type** is a formal description of the kind of data used in a computer program.

How an item of data is stored and manipulated in the computer depends on its data type. This is why it is important to clearly define the data type of any items of data you use in a program. When the item of data is a variable, then defining the data type is called 'declaring the variable'.

Exactly how a variable is declared will vary from language to language, but usually you will need to state:

- an identifier (name) for the variable
- the data type of the variable.

This causes the computer to allocate some memory of the correct size for this variable, and associate this memory location with the identifier given. In the rest of the code, the identifier is used to refer to the data stored in that memory location.

Common data types used in programming languages include numeric data types, alphanumeric data types and Booleans.

Numeric data types

Numeric data types are used to store numbers. They are usually stored by converting the number into binary (see Chapter 3.1).

The most commonly used numeric data types are integer and real. Their typical use is shown in the table on the next page.

	Used to store	Typical size	Notes
Integer	Whole Numbers	2 or 4 bytes	The different size of integers are sometimes called short integer (2 bytes) and long integer (4 bytes). Some systems also provide a 1-byte integer used to store numbers either ranging from 0 to 255, or from -128 to +127.
Real	Numbers that may have a decimal point	4 or 8 bytes	Real numbers are also sometimes called **floating point numbers**. You will study details of how they are represented in Chapter 16.2.

Some systems will also include specialised numeric data types such as Date/Time and Currency.

Alphanumeric data types

Alphanumeric data types are used to store textual data. They are used to store characters, digits and punctuation symbols.

The most basic alphanumeric data type is the **Character**. This stores only one character or digit or symbol and typically has a size of 1 byte.

More often, we want to store and manipulate longer text than just one character (for example a person's name). For this purpose, most programming languages provide a data type **String** that consists of a string of characters grouped under one identifier.

Each character usually takes a byte, so the length of a string is the number of characters stored in it. However, the length of a variable of type string should be the length of the longest string that you intend to store in that variable.

Note that alphanumeric data types are used for items of data which appear to be numbers, when it is the characters (digits) in the number and not their value which is important. This has been discussed in Chapter 3.1.

A typical example is a telephone number. The value of the telephone number 029830001 is not one more than the telephone number 023830000. They are just different telephone numbers. If you take the leading 0 off and dial 29830001 you will not get the same result. This is because what is important is each character in the telephone number, not the value of the telephone number as a whole. Therefore a telephone number should be stored as a String (a sequence of digits) rather than as a number.

Other examples of such 'pseudo-numbers' include various reference numbers such as customer/product numbers, credit card numbers and the ISBN number of books. Occasionally, these numbers even contain non-digit characters such as dashes, brackets and spaces that clearly show that they are alphanumeric.

Booleans

Boolean data is data that can only have two values. The two possible values are often referred to as TRUE and FALSE. They are also sometimes referred to as 1(TRUE) and 0(False) or YES and NO.

Boolean data is often used to store whether or not an event has occurred or a condition has been met. For this reason, they are sometimes called Flags (a reference to the flags on American mailboxes which are Up when there is mail in the mailbox, and Down when there is no mail – a Boolean quantity).

Booleans are typically stored in one byte for convenience. One bit is sufficient to store the data, but computers find it easier to deal with whole bytes.

2. Data structures

Data structures allow us to store more than one item of data together under one identifier (name) which can then be used to access the individual items of data if necessary.

Two data structures we shall look at are **Arrays** and **Records**.

Arrays

An array contains several items of similar data.

For example, the number of votes for each candidate in an election will be an integer. Supposing there are four candidates, we could store these votes in four separate variables:

    VotesForCandidate1
    VotesForCandidate2
    VotesForCandidate3
    VotesForCandidate4

However, it is better to use an array called VotesForCandidate that contains all four integers. The individual integers can now be referred to as:

    VotesForCandidate(1)
    VotesForCandidate(2)
    VotesForCandidate(3)
    VotesForCandidate(4)

Such an array can be represented in a table as shown below:

VotesForCandidate

1	2	3	4
2300	1091	105	7891

The second row of this table shows the actual data that is stored in memory. These are the **elements** of the array. Because the elements are all of the same data type, they will take the same amount of space in memory and are usually stored next to each other.

The first row of the table tells us the position of each item of the array. This is called the **index**. As all the elements have the same size, the computer can use the index to calculate the position of each element in the array. This allows the computer to use the index to access each element directly using the name and the index.

For example, the value of VotesForCandidate(2) in the example above is 1091.

The lowest and highest values of the index are the **bounds** of the array. In the example, the lower bound is 1, and the upper bound is 4. In some languages, the lower bound of arrays (the index of the first element) defaults to 1. In other languages it defaults to 0.

Using an array to store related data has advantages over using separate variables:

- You declare all the elements in one statement. If the number of elements changes, all you need to do is change the bounds of the array in the declaration.
- Because the array contains similar data, you can use a loop to perform similar operations on all elements of the array. For example, to print all the elements in our example:

```
For i = 1 to 4
  OUTPUT Candidate",i,"had",VotesForCandidate(i),
  "votes."
Next i
```

The array VotesForCandidate is a one-dimensional list of elements. Each element therefore has only one index.

Arrays can also be multi-dimensional. For example, a two-dimensional array will be like a table, and each element will have two indices, to indicate which row and which column it is in the table.

A two-dimensional array called A can be represented in a table, such as the one shown below:

	1	2	3	4
1	23	11	21	25
2	10	77	15	18
3	35	10	28	83

The element in the first row and second column of this array is 11. If we define the rows as the first dimension, and the columns as the second dimension, then the element in the first row and second column is given by A(1,2).

To declare this array, we would use:

```
DIM A(1 to 3, 1 to 4) : Integer
```

(Once again, remember that the exact code used to declare an array will vary from language to language.)

We can use nested loops to do similar operations to each element of the array. For example, to set every element of the array to 0:

```
01  FOR Row = 1 to 3
02    FOR Column = 1 to 4
03      A(Row, Column) = 0
04    NEXT Column
05  Next Row
```

Records

We saw that the arrays are useful for storing a series of similar data items together under one identifier.

Sometimes we need to store several different data items under one identifier, because they are all related to a particular individual or object in real life. For example, a school might store the name, gender and age of each student. It makes sense to keep these items together.

Records can be used to store such items. In our example, we could define a record for students as follows:

```
RECORD Student
  Name : String
  Gender : Character
  Age : Integer
END RECORD
```

The exact code for defining a record will vary from language to language.

The individual items of data inside the record are called **fields**. So the Student record has three fields that are called Name, Gender and Age.

To design a record format means to decide which fields are needed in the record for a particular application. By adding up the size in bytes of each of the fields in a record, you can calculate the size of the record.

The data in a file usually consists of a number of records, each record relating to one individual, object, etc. in real life. By knowing the number of records there are in the file and the size of the records, it is possible to calculate the size of the file.

In code, a record format which has been defined can be used to declare variables to represent each record. The fields of the record can then be accessed through these variables. The code below defines a student and assigns values to its records:

```
DIM TheStudent as Student
TheStudent.Name = "Frida Smith"
TheStudent.Gender = "F"
TheStudent.Age = 16
```

3. File organisation

We saw in the previous section that files consist of a series of records. In this section we shall look at how the records are organised in the file.

Serial file

In a **serial file**, the data is stored in the order in which it arrives.

New data is simply added to the end of the file. This is called **appending** the data.

If an item of data is to be deleted, this will create a gap in the file. This can be removed by recreating the file: copying all the records in the file, apart from the record to be deleted, into a new file and using this file to replace the original file.

To search for data in a serial file, you will need to start from the first item and search for each item in turn until you find the record you are looking for. If the item you are searching for is not in the file, you will need to search every item in the file before you can be certain that the item is not found.

Sequential file

In a **sequential file**, the data are stored according to a key field in the data. The key field is a field in each record that can be used to identify the record. For example, if each student were given a StudentID, then a sequential file of students will be stored in order of the Student ID.

The addition of an item to a sequential file requires the new item to be inserted within the existing records. This is usually achieved by recreating the file. All the records up to the correct point of insertion are copied to a new file. The new record is then appended in the correct position and the remaining records are copied into the new file. The new file then replaces the old file.

If an item is deleted this would create a gap in the sequence. This can be prevented by recreating the file in the same manner as deleting an item from a serial file.

Searching for an item in a sequential file is usually similar to searching for an item in a serial file. You start from the first item and you search each item in turn until you reach the item you are searching for. However, if you reach an item that has a higher value for the key than the item you are searching for, then you do not need to carry on searching till the end of the file to know that the item is not found.

Indexed sequential files

An **indexed sequential file** is a sequential file where the data is arranged according to a key field in the record, but which also has an index that allows the records to be found directly.

This is useful in files where sometimes it is necessary to process all records in sequential order, and sometimes it is necessary to access individual records. For example, if the program is printing a register of the students in a student file then it will access the data sequentially. However, if you want to look up the details of an individual student, then the index is used to find the required record quickly.

Direct-access files

> Note: **Direct-access files** are sometimes also called **random-access files**. These should not be confused with random files. Records in a direct-access file are stored next to each other and are accessed by using their position within the file. Records in a random file are stored separately, each at the address calculated by a hash algorithm. This address is used to retrieve the record.

If the records in a sequential file have a fixed length then it may be possible to read the contents of any record in the file directly if you know its position in the file. For example if the size of a record is 40 bytes, then the records in the file will be at positions 0, 40, 80, 120, etc. To find the tenth record, it is not necessary to go through all the records in the file. The position or 'address' of the record can be calculated using the following formula:

Address of Record number n = beginning of file + ((n-1) * Size of record)

In this case the tenth record will be at position 360.

Random files

In all the file types we have discussed so far, the records are physically stored next to each other either serially or sequentially. A random file allows the data to be stored anywhere in a dedicated section of a disk. A calculation called a **hash algorithm** is performed on a field in the record to be stored. The result of this calculation then becomes the address. As a result, the records can appear randomly scattered across the disk. However, finding the data is extremely quick as long as you know the key field and the hash algorithm. There is no need to refer to the other data in the file. As a result, random files are very useful for large databases where individual records are often looked up individually.

Estimating the size of a file

It is possible to estimate the size of a data file using the number of records in the file and the sizes of the fields in each record. The procedure is as follows:

- Determine the size, in bytes, of each field in the record (for a string field, use the largest size allowed).
- Add the field sizes to calculate the size of one record.
- Multiply the size of one record by the number of records in the file.
- Add 10% to the result, for additional storage that will be needed to manage the file on the disk (we call this **overheads**).

This will give you an estimate of the size of the file in bytes. If necessary, it can be converted into kilobytes (kB) by dividing by 1024, and then converted again into megabytes (MB) by dividing again by 1024. (This is because there are 1024 bytes in a kilobyte and 1024 kilobytes in a megabyte). However, for the purposes of estimating, dividing by 1000 instead of 1024 would give a reasonably adequate result.

For example, suppose a school had 1800 students and kept their details in a file of records structured as follows:

```
RECORD Student
  Name : String
  Gender : Character
  Age : Integer
END RECORD
```

The size of each field can be given by:

Field	Data type	Size
Name	String	20
Gender	Character	1
Age	Integer	2

The total size of each record is 23 bytes.

The size of 1800 records is therefore $23 \times 1800 = 41{,}400$ bytes.

Adding 10% for overheads gives us $41{,}400 \times 1.1 = 45{,}540$ bytes.

Dividing this by 1000 gives us an estimate of 45.5 kB.

File handling operations

To write programs that deal with data in files, a programmer needs to know some basic file operations and how they are implemented in the language being used.

We discuss the principles of the main file operations here. The way these principles are implemented in different programming languages varies.

Preparing the file: most languages will require the program to make the operating system aware that a file is about to be used. This is often done using an OPEN command. When the file is opened it is often necessary to specify how the file is going to be used (e.g. read only, read and write data, write data only, append to existing data, direct access, etc.). This is called the **access mode**. It protects the data in the file from being corrupted, for example, by conflicting instructions using the same file. For this reason, it is good practice to open a file for as little time as necessary. When the operation is over, the file should be closed. This releases the file so that it can be used by another part of the program, or another program.

Reading data from a file: languages provide different methods for reading data. The simplest way is to read the data from the file one line at a time. This is useful for searching through a serial file. In this case it is necessary to test, before reading each line, that the end of the file has not been reached. For random and direct-access files, you need to be able to read the data that is at a given address in the file.

Writing data to a file: you also need to be able to write the data into a file that has been correctly opened. This can include replacing (updating) the data in a direct-access file, or adding data to the end of a serial file (appending). Inserting data into a sequential file will require all subsequent records to be moved to make space for the data to be inserted. An alternative method is to create a new file and copy all the records from the present file into it, inserting the new data in the file at the correct location. The new file then replaces the old file. This is called **merging** the data into the sequential file. The example below for deleting a record from a sequential file uses a similar technique.

File management: programming languages also provide facilities for copying, moving, deleting files, and finding out if a file exists.

The following algorithm uses several of the file operations discussed to delete a record from a sequential file:

```
BEGIN
  Open SourceFile for reading
  Create NewFile
  Open NewFile for writing
REPEAT
  Read a record from SourceFile
  IF it is not the record you want to delete THEN
   Write the record to NewFile
  END IF
UNTIL end of sourcefile

Close SourceFile
Close NewFile

Delete SourceFile
Rename NewFile to the name of the SourceFile
END
```

END OF CHAPTER QUESTIONS

1   A supermarket stock control system stores details of the items of stock that the supermarket has for sale.

Data stored about each item includes:
- price
- number left in stock
- size of item (S for small, M for medium and L for large)
- whether or not a delivery of new stock is expected.

(a) Explain what is meant by each of the following data types and state an item of data from the stock file that would be stored using it:
   (i)   Boolean
   (ii) Character
   (iii) Integer
   (iv) Real Number.   (8)

2 A secretary of a swimming club keeps a file of information about the members of the club. The club has 1000 members. The information held is shown in the table:

Field	Data type	Estimated size (in bytes)
Member surname		
Date of birth		
Time in seconds for 100 metres		
Whether in team		

(a) Complete the table to show data types and sizes for each of the fields. (5)

(b) Estimate the size of the file, giving your answer in appropriate units. (3)

[OCR AS Computing paper 2506 – June 2006]

3 An estate agency stores details of houses in a computer system.

(a) Define the following data types and state a piece of information about each house which would be stored using that data type:

Data type	Information stored
Character	
Integer	
Boolean	

(b) By referring to the information held by the estate agent, explain what is meant by a:

(i) record (2)

(ii) field. (2)

[OCR AS Computing paper 2506 – June 2006]

4 This question is about different types of access to data held in storage.

(a) A bank holds a file of customer account details. This file is used in the production of monthly statements for customers.

Explain why this file is accessed sequentially. (2)

(b) Customers expect to be able to enquire about the details of their accounts over the telephone.

(i) Explain why sequential access to data is **not** suitable for this. (2)

(ii) State a more suitable type of access to the data, justifying your answer. (2)

(c) Customer transactions are stored on a temporary file in the order in which they occur.

State a type of file access most suitable for the data in this file, justifying your answer. (2)

[OCR AS Computing paper 2506 – June 2006]

5   (a) State three items that need to be specified when declaring an array.   (3)

    (b) The number of students in each tutor group in a school is stored in a two-dimensional 5 by 3 array
        of integers called TutorGroupSize. There are 5 year groups, and 3 tutor groups in each year group.
        Write an algorithm to calculate the total number of students in the school, by adding all the values
        in the array.

6   An arcade game keeps the 25 highest scores in a sequential file in rank order. When a new high score is
    achieved, it is placed inside the file in the correct position. Other scores may have to be adjusted or
    deleted as a result.

    (a) State what appending an item to a file means.   (1)

    (b) Explain why new high scores cannot always be appended to the high-score file.   (2)

    (c) Write an algorithm to insert a new high score into its correct position in a file that already
        contains 25 high scores.   (6)

Chapter 10 Common Facilities of Programming Languages

In this chapter we discuss the operations and functions that are built into most languages and that are used to manipulate the data in the program. We focus on the most common operations, which provide a useful basis for learning the more advanced features of any programming language.

These include:

- the assignment operation
- operations on numbers
- string manipulation operations and functions
- input and output.

1. The assignment operator

Programs use variables that can be given different values while the program is running. The operation of setting an actual value to a variable is called **assignment**.

The assignment operator is usually the equals sign (=) and a typical assignment operation uses the following format:

<variable> = <expression>

For example, if x and y are variables, we can have:

x = 7
y = 3 * (5 + 2)

In these examples, the value of 7 will be stored in the variable x, and the value of 21 will be stored in the variable y.

There are two important things to note about the assignment operator.

Firstly, it should not be confused with the equality operator which we shall see later, and which sometimes also uses the equals sign (=). For this reason, it is often helpful to read the assignment operator as 'becomes' rather than 'equals'. So the operation x = 7 would be read as 'x becomes 7'.

In some languages, to avoid this confusion, a different sign such as := is used for the assignment operator. However, many languages use the same sign because the computer can tell from the code that the programmer wants to assign a value to a variable. An assignment statement is usually a complete instruction in itself. An equality operator can only be used within an expression and not as an instruction in itself.

The second thing to note is that the assignment operator is not commutative. This means that you cannot swap the left-hand side and the right-hand side of the operator. For example, you cannot write 7 = x. (This would read as '7 becomes x', which is clearly nonsense). The left-hand side of an assignment operator must be a single variable. The right-hand side must be an expression that can be a single value, or a complex expression that evaluates to a single value.

2. Arithmetic operations

Arithmetic operations are used to manipulate numeric data (integers and real numbers) and produce a result. The numbers that are to be manipulated are called **operands**. You will be familiar with arithmetic operations from your study of Mathematics. They include operations such as + (addition) and * (multiplication).

A significant difference between arithmetic operations and the assignment operation is that while assignment operators perform an action in the program (i.e. change the value of a variable) an arithmetic operation only tells us how to manipulate the data. It does not tell us what to do with the result. This means that an arithmetic operation cannot be an instruction or a program statement on its own. It can only be used as an expression in a statement that tells the computer what to do with the result.

Some operators have only one operand. These are called **unary operators** and the operator is usually written before the operand. Other operators have two operands. These are called **binary operators** and the operator is usually written between the two operands. (Other variations are possible. In Chapter 19.2 of Unit 3, we discuss a notation where operators are written after the operands.)

Note that the same operator symbol can mean different operations depending on the context. Consider the following two expressions:

$-m$

$n - m$

In the first expression the – sign is the unary operator for *negation*. The result of the expression is the negative of the value of m. In the second operation the – sign is the binary operator for *subtraction*. The result of the operation is the value of m subtracted from the value of n.

Division

If you add, subtract or multiply integers, the result will be an integer. This is not the case for the division operation. For example, 13 divided by 5 can only be expressed as a real number (2.6) or two integers (2 remainder 3). Many programming languages therefore allow for a number of operators to perform divisions on integers. These are summarised in the following table:

Operation	Usual symbol	Meaning	Examples
Ordinary (Real) Division	/	A normal division operation; the result is a real number, even when the operands are integers.	13 / 5 = 2.6 15 / 3 = 5.0 2 / 9 = 0.222 ...
Quotient (Integer Division)	DIV (sometimes % or \)	The operands are integers, and the result is the integer part of the result.	13 DIV 5 = 2 15 DIV 3 = 5 2 DIV 9 = 0
Remainder (Modulo arithmetic)	MOD	The operands are integers and the result is the remainder when the first number is divided by the second.	13 MOD 5 = 3 15 MOD 3 = 0 2 MOD 9 = 2

3. Relational operations

Relational operators compare data and produce a result of TRUE or FALSE depending on how the data compared relate to each other. Because they are used to compare data, they are also called **comparison operators**.

The most common relational operators are:

= (or ==)	Is equal to
<> (or !=)	Is not equal to
<	Is less than
>	Is greater than
<=	Is less than or equal to
>=	Is greater than or equal to

Different languages will use variations of these symbols.

These operations are all binary, and the operator is written between the operands. The operands should be of the same data type so that they can be compared with each other. The result of the operation is always a Boolean – either TRUE or FALSE. For this reason, relational operations are very useful for the conditions of IF statements and condition-controlled loops.

4. Boolean operations

Boolean operators combine operands that are of Boolean data type, and the result is a Boolean. They are also called **logical operators**.

The three main operators are AND, OR and NOT.

Their operation is often described using truth tables that show all the possible combinations of operands and their result.

The AND operation has two operands. The result is TRUE if both operands are TRUE. Otherwise the result is FALSE.

a	b	Result of (a AND b)
FALSE	FALSE	FALSE
FALSE	TRUE	FALSE
TRUE	FALSE	FALSE
TRUE	TRUE	TRUE

The OR operator also has two operands. The result is TRUE if either of the operands is TRUE, and it is FALSE if both the operands are FALSE.

a	b	Result of (a OR b)
FALSE	FALSE	FALSE
FALSE	TRUE	TRUE
TRUE	FALSE	TRUE
TRUE	TRUE	TRUE

The NOT operator only has one operand. The result is TRUE if the operand is FALSE and vice versa.

a	Result of NOT a
FALSE	TRUE
TRUE	FALSE

5. Operator precedence

Operations can be put together to make complex expressions. When this is done, the computer needs to know the order in which to carry out the operations. For example, consider the following statement:

x = 3 + 5 * 6

There are three operations, an assignment (=), an addition (+) and a multiplication (*). If the addition is done before the multiplication, x will be assigned to 48. In your studies of Mathematics you have learnt that this is not the usual way that the expression is evaluated. This is due to **operator precedence**. Multiplication has a higher precedence than addition, and so it should be carried out first. (Notice that the assignment operator has the lowest precedence, so it did not try to assign x to the value 3, which would have caused an error.)

The usual precedence of the operations we have discussed is given in the table below. We will consider items on the same row to have the same order of precedence:

Unary Operators	– (negation), NOT
Multiplication and Division	*, /, DIV, MOD
Addition and Subtraction	+, –
Comparison operators	<, >, <=, =>, = (equality), <>
Boolean operators (except NOT)	AND, OR
Assignment	= (assignment)

When operators have the same precedence, they are usually evaluated from left to right. For example, in 6 – 3 + 1, 6 – 3 is evaluated first and the answer is 4. If 3 + 1 was evaluated first the answer would be 2.

Parentheses or brackets can be used to change the order of precedence. Any items in brackets should be evaluated first. If there is more than one set of brackets, then they are evaluated in turn from the innermost to the outermost.

For example, let's consider the following statement once again:

x = 3 + 5 * 6

In order to do the addition first we must put it in brackets, as items in brackets have to be done first:

x = (3 + 5) * 6

Note that it is good practice to use brackets even when the order of precedence will perform the operations in the correct order, if it makes the expression easier to understand. So it is good practice to write:

$$x = 3 + (5 * 6)$$

6. String manipulation

As many programs need to deal with text, most programming languages provide operations and functions that manipulate strings. We shall discuss a few of the most common string operations.

Concatenating

To **concatenate** two strings means to join them together to make one string. Many languages use the operator + for this operation, as it is similar to adding the two strings together to make a bigger string.

Consider the following statement, where FullName, FirstName and Surname are string variables:

FullName = FirstName + Surname

If the value of FirstName is 'Mike' and the value of Surname is 'Banks' then the variable FullName would be assigned to 'MikeBanks'. This is probably not what was intended. A better version of that statement would also concatenate a space between the two variables, as follows:

FullName = FirstName + " " + Surname"

Extracting parts of a string

Most languages have built-in functions to extract part of a string. They are often called LEFT, RIGHT or MID, depending on which part of the string the letters need to be extracted from.

Here is a common format for the use of these functions in many languages:

LEFT

FORMAT	LEFT(<string>,<number of characters>)
What it does	returns the given number of characters from the left of the string
Example	LEFT("mathematics",3) returns the string "mat"

RIGHT

FORMAT	RIGHT(<string>, <number of characters>)
What it does	returns the given number of characters from the right of the string
Example	RIGHT("mathematics",4) will return the string "tics"

MID

FORMAT	MID(<string>,<starting position>,<number of characters>)
What it does	returns the given number of characters from the given starting position
Example	MID("mathematics",3,4) returns the string "them"

Locating

Another common requirement is to search a string for another (shorter) string. This is usually done using a function built into the language sometimes called LOCATE, FIND or POSITION_OF.

One possible format for this function is:

LOCATE(<search string>,<main string>)

This will try to find the search string inside the main string. If the string is found, then it will return an integer, which is the position of the search string inside the main string. If the string is not found, it typically returns the number 0. So, LOCATE("the", "mathematics") would return 3 (as "the" can be found from the third character of "mathematics"), but LOCATE ("tea","mathematics") would return 0.

> Note: The use of this function varies greatly between languages.

One issue is what to return if the search string occurs more than once, as in LOCATE("at","mathematics"). Many languages will return 2, the position of the *first* occurrence. Although the function varies between languages, the main principle of locating the position of a string within another is the same.

Finding the length of a string

Most languages have a function to determine the length of a string, which has a format such as:

LENGTH(<string>)

This function returns an integer that is the length (the number of characters) in the string. For example LENGTH("mathematics") will return the integer 11.

Dealing with character codes

As we saw in Chapter 8.1 strings are made up of characters, and each character is represented in the computer by a numeric character code.

It is often useful to know the code of a given character or vice versa. This can be done using built-in functions such as:

CHAR(<character code>) which returns the character that has the given character code.

ASCII(<character>) that returns the character code (in this case the ASCII code) of the given character.

< Activity >

ROT13 is an encryption code often used on web pages to hide the punch lines of jokes and other information that the reader may not want to read unless they choose to. Letters A to M are replaced by the letter in the alphabet which is 13 places ahead of them, and letters N to Z are replaced by the letter which is 13 places behind.

Here is an algorithm for a function that takes a string of uppercase characters A–Z and encrypts it using ROT13. It uses many of the string manipulation functions we have discussed:

```
FUNCTION Convert(OldString:String) :
  String
  StringLength = LENGTH(OldString)
  Position = 0
  NewString = ""
  FOR Position = 1 TO StringLength
    OldCharacter =
Mid(OldString,Position,1)
    OldCode = ASCII(OldCharacter)
    IF OldCode < ASCII("N") THEN
      NewCode = OldCode + 13
    ELSE
      NewCode = OldCode - 13
    END IF
    NewCharacter = CHAR(NewCode)
    NewString = NewString + NewCharacter
  NEXT Position
  RETURN NewString
END FUNCTION
```

1 Identify the string manipulation functions that have been used in this algorithm.
2 Write comments explaining what the computer does at each step of the algorithm.
3 Implement the algorithm in a high level language. You will need to adapt the algorithm so that you are using functions available in the language you have chosen.

Comparing strings

We have already said that strings are made up of characters that are represented by their numeric character code. When you use comparison operators with strings, many languages just perform an alphanumeric comparison.

This means that the codes of the characters are compared in turn, starting from the first character, to decide which string is greater. If the first characters have the same code, then the next characters are compared, and so on. This is like putting words in alphabetical order, except that it is using the whole character set of the alphabet instead of just the letters A to Z.

This can cause unexpected results in many programs where strings are compared with each other. For example, upper and lower case characters do not have the same character code, so the comparison "Bob" = "bob" would result in FALSE, making such comparisons case-sensitive. Also, where a string contains digits then "11" will be considered to be less than "2" because the code of the first character is lower.

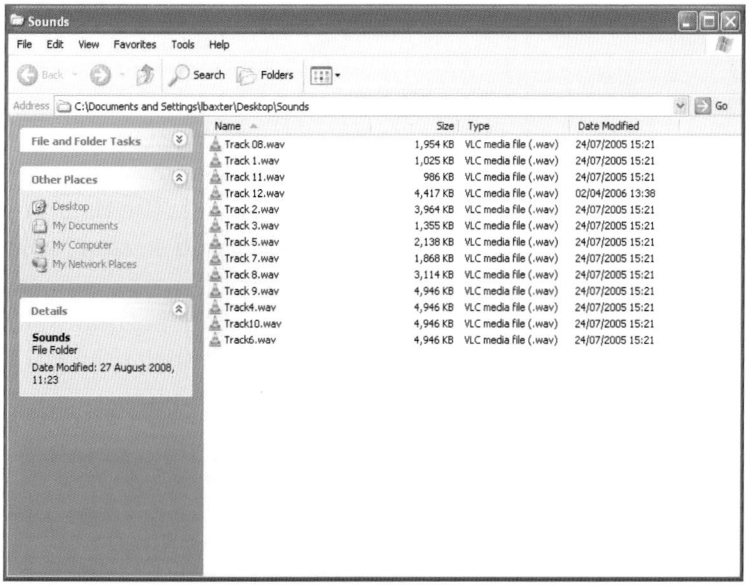

Figure 2.15 The DOS command "dir /B /ON" lists the names of the files in the current directory in alphabetical order. Notice how sorting strings according to character codes can lead to unexpected results

It is obviously impractical to learn the character codes of every character in a character set. But it is useful to know that in most character sets, the general order of the most common characters (from lowest to highest code) is as shown in the table below:

The SPACE character (and most common punctuation symbols)
Digits 0–9 in order
Uppercase letters A–Z in order
Lowercase letters a–z in order
Letters with accents such as é

Any programmer writing a program that compares strings needs to be aware of how strings are compared in the language used to ensure that the correct results are obtained. Here are some strategies for making sure the right comparison is made:

- Some languages have options for deciding how strings are compared (e.g. you can set an option asking the program to make string searches not case-sensitive). Use these options where available.
- Ensure that strings compared are in a consistent format. This includes the length of the string and the position of characters. This would allow postcodes such as "N 1 3AA" and "N13 2AA" to be sorted correctly.
- Add leading 0s or spaces to numeric strings. For example, "10" is less than "2", but it is greater than "02".
- Validation (see Chapter 3.2) can be used to ensure that when the data is input, it is already in a format that will be compared correctly.
- Replace accented characters (for the purpose of comparing and sorting) with non-accented equivalents. For example, replace "Zoë" with "Zoe", as "Zoë" would come after words such as "Zoo" in an alphanumeric comparison.

7. Input and output facilities

As we saw in Chapter 7.1 a program normally allows the user to input data, process the data in some way and output the result. We have discussed several facilities in languages that allow us to manipulate or process the data. It would however be impossible to write any useful programs, unless we could also input and output data. We shall now discuss some of the facilities and methods for doing this.

How the data is input or output will depend on:

- the type of user interface (for example graphical, menu or command-based)
- the input and output devices available.

Graphical user interfaces use a variety of user interface objects such as textboxes, drop-down lists, option boxes and check boxes to allow the users to input data. Choosing the most appropriate object for the item of data that needs to be input can allow for validation. For example, if the data to be input is one of a small set of possibilities such as a person's gender or marital status, then a restricted drop-down list would be better than a textbox as it would ensure that only valid data can be entered.

When user interface objects are used to input and output data, it is important to be aware of the data types of the data being used. For example, the data type of the contents of a textbox is usually a string. If you are using the textbox to input an integer, for example a person's height in cm, then you should be aware that the program may treat the value in the textbox as a string rather than an integer. This is illustrated in Figure 2.16 (an algorithm to calculate BMI, or Body Mass Index).

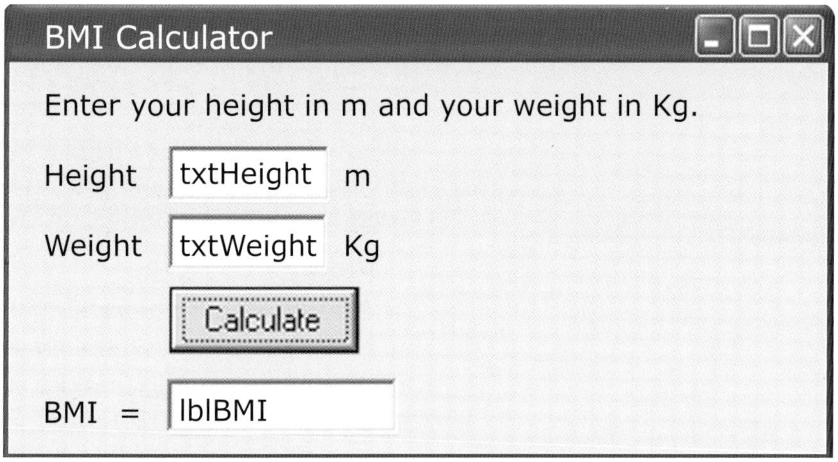

Figure 2.16

The algorithm for the calculate command could be written as:

```
01  BEGIN Calculate
02    lblBMI = txtWeight / (txtHeight * txtHeight)
03  END
```

By acting directly on the user interface objects, this algorithm will try to perform arithmetic operations on the contents of the textboxes, which are strings by definition. This might produce incorrect results in some languages, especially if the user is allowed to enter strings into the textboxes that are not valid numbers.

A better algorithm would use specific statements to input the data from textboxes and store them into variables that are of the correct data type, as shown below:

```
01  BEGIN Calculate
02    Declare Height, Weight and BMI as Real numbers
03    Set Height to the contents of txtHeight
04    Set Weight to the contents of txtWeight
05    BMI = Weight / (Height * Height)
06    Set the caption of lblBMI to BMI
07  END
```

This algorithm now has specific statements for input (lines 02 and 03) and output (line 06). Separating the input and output from the processing in this way has another advantage. You can change the interface without affecting the code that processes the data. You only need to change the statements that deal with input and output.

Dialogue boxes are windows that appear on the screen to allow easy input and output of specific data at a given point in the program. They are usually **modal**. This means that the user cannot continue running the program until the dialogue has been closed. Programming languages usually offer a range of standard dialogues. Two commonly used standard dialogues are the message box or alert, which is used to output one item of data, and the input dialogue or input box which typically allows the program to output a prompt or question and then input the user's answer to this prompt. Other standard dialogue boxes are used to set up the printer or save a file. The programmer may also create custom dialogue boxes for the needs of the program.

The results of the program may need to be output to a printer or to a file rather than on screen. Most languages will allow the programmer to write text directly to the printer in the same way. You could think of the printer as a file, except that instead of storing the data on a disk, it stores it on paper.

Many languages offer a facility to display lines of text neatly, separating and justifying the words and setting numerical values and dates to a specified pattern or format. This is called **pretty printing**. Pretty printing facilities are useful when outputting data to a text file or a printer, especially tabular data. Where pretty printing facilities are not provided in a language, the string manipulation facilities can be used to achieve the same effect.

Instead of sending text directly to the printer, some languages allow the programmer to define a report layout which specifies what data should be printed and in what position. The program can then provide the data onto the predefined format and send the report to the printer.

END OF CHAPTER QUESTIONS

1   Evaluate the following expressions:
   (a) 17 MOD 3   (b) 3 * 5 = 14
   (c) NOT (– 3 < 0)   (d) 12 + 30 DIV 4   (4)

2   Some of the following statements contain errors in the use of the operators. For each statement, state whether there is an error, giving a reason for your answer. If there is no error, your reason should explain what the statement would do.

   (a) `x = (y = 3)`

   (b) `PI * r * r = A`

   (c) `s = LENGTH(CustomerName * 3)`

(d)

```
IF x = 2 OR 3 THEN
    OUTPUT "Too Low"
END IF
```
(8)

3   The software for a telephone company includes a function that takes the duration of a call as a string and returns the length of the call in minutes. For example, if the input is "1:30" the output will be 1.5.

Here is an algorithm for this function:

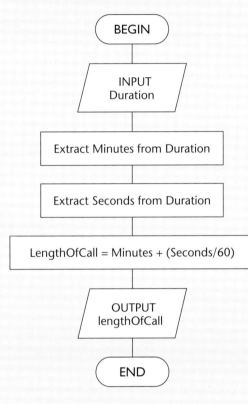

Using the string manipulation and input–output facilities of a high level programming language, write the code for this function according to the algorithm given. You should state the name of the language you are using.

(8)

Chapter 11 Writing Maintainable Programs

In this chapter we will discuss techniques for writing code using good programming style. The programme writing techniques explored here should be practised as soon as a person first learns to program.

Many of these techniques are conventions that are accepted and used by good programmers across the world. Using them will ensure that your code will be easily understood and therefore easy to maintain if it needs to be debugged or improved in the future.

1. The importance of good programming style

Good programming style allows the program code to be easily understood when it is read. This has many advantages:

■ Good programming techniques enable the programmer to focus on what the program is intended to do and makes it easier to check that the program actually does it, because the intention is spelt out in the comments alongside the code. It also provides an easy reference to data that the programmer needs to be aware of when writing the code. As a result, fewer errors are made.
■ Programmers often work in a team. Consistently using good programming style allows all the members in the team to understand each other's code and ensure that the modules they have written are compatible with modules written by other team members. Other team members can also maintain the code, for example if the original programmer has left the team.
■ Similarly, the programmers who wrote the code may need to revisit it after a period of time, or after they have worked on a different program. Usually this is due to a maintenance issue because the code has got to be amended to repair bugs or add new features. Good programming style will reduce the time needed for the programmers to familiarise themselves again with the code, which will increase their overall productivity.

2. Variables and constants

Most procedural languages allow you to define and use **variables** and **constants**. We have already used variables in previous chapters. In this chapter we focus on how using variables and constants, including naming them correctly, can make code easier to understand.

A **variable** is a name used to refer to a particular memory location that is used to store data. The value of the data held in that memory location can change while the program is running. The main purpose of a variable is to allow the programmer to write code that manipulates the data without knowing yet what the data will be.

A **constant** is a name used to refer to a fixed value. The value is set when the code is written and cannot be changed while the program is running. The main purpose of a constant is to make code easier to read and to maintain.

The name of a variable or constant is also called its **identifier**.

Selecting identifiers

Most languages insist that identifiers must begin with a letter but otherwise can contain letters, digits and a few other characters such as underscores.

Here are some issues to be considered when selecting identifiers for a variable or a constant:

- When declaring variables and constants, the programmer should use meaningful identifiers that communicate their purpose. Single letter identifiers should be avoided. (An exception can be made for i, j and k, which are conventionally used as control variables in a loop).
- As spaces are not allowed, make the division between words clear within an identifier name by using underscores or by using uppercase letters at the start of a new word. For example 'time_of_arrival', or 'TimeOfArrival' are both easier to read than 'timeofarrival'.
- Use prefixes at the start of identifier names to remind you of the data type of the variable. For example, if a programmer reads strMessage or iAge in a piece of code, they will know immediately that Message is a string, and Age is an integer. There are different conventions for using prefixes like this. Only one convention should be used in any one program.
- Reserved words (or keywords) are words that are already used in the programming language for a specific purpose. They include control structures (such as IF, END) as well as built-in operations and functions (such as OR and PRINT). These cannot be used as identifiers.

Scope

When declaring a variable or a constant, the programmer needs to be aware of its **scope**. This is usually local or global.

A **local variable** is declared and used inside a module or subroutine and is only available in that module. It is created when the subroutine is called and destroyed when the subroutine exits.

A **global variable** is declared at the beginning of the code and is available throughout the code, including all its subroutines.

It is good programming style to use local variables as far as possible. This prevents the data of different subroutines interfering with each other, if the same names have been used. Global variables should only be used because the data needs to be preserved each time the subroutine is called, or because the data is needed by several subroutines.

Initialising variables

Some programming languages will **initialise** variables when they are declared. This means that the variables are given a starting value. Typically, integers are set to 0, Booleans are set to FALSE and strings are set to the empty string. If this initial value is assumed in the code, then it makes the logic of the code more difficult to understand. For example, consider the following algorithm that allows the user to input 5 numbers and outputs their total:

```
BEGIN
  FOR i = 1 to 5
   INPUT Number
   Total = Total + Number
  NEXT i
  OUTPUT Total
END
```

This algorithm is logically incomplete because it can only work if the value of Total is 0 to begin with. If the system automatically sets this, the program will work. However, initialising Total explicitly by inserting the line Total = 0 as the first statement, makes the code easier to understand.

As a rule, the first time any variable is used, it should be on the left-hand side of an assignment statement.

Using constants

Constants can be very useful in making code easier to read and maintain. Many programs contain values that do not change while the program is running. These may be universal constants that are always the same, such as the value of Pi, or values that refer to the specific program, such as the name of the font used by screen objects.

New programmers tend to use literals in their code for such values. This means that the code contains the actual values spelt out in full. For example:

```
Circumference = 3.14159266 * Diameter
Label1.Font = "Arial"
Label2.Font = "Arial"
Label3.Font = "Arial"
```

As a general rule, the programmer should avoid using literals in code and substitute them with constants unless there is a good reason not to do so.

In the example above, we could declare two constants:

```
CONSTANT PI = 3.14159266
CONSTANT DefaultFont = "Ariel"
```

The code would then become:

```
Circumference = PI * Diameter
Label1.Font = DefaultFont
Label2.Font = DefaultFont
Label3.Font = DefaultFont
```

This code is immediately more understandable. Also, if the programmer wanted to change the default font, the change needs only to be made in the declaration, rather than every time the value is used, making the code easier to maintain.

3. Code layout

The way in which the code is written also contributes significantly to making it more maintainable. This includes organising the code into modules, using indentation to show the control structures within the module and using white space to format the code into logical groups of statements.

Modularised code

To make the code easier to understand, the code should be written as a series of small routines that can quickly be seen to be performing one function. Complex operations should be broken up into subroutines that are defined separately and called from the main routine. **Modularisation** is easier to achieve if the program has been designed using top-down techniques.

Indentation

The use of **indentation** has already been discussed in Chapter 8.3. Every time a code structure is used which has a beginning and an ending statement on separate lines, the code within the structure should be given a new level of indentation. There should be a strip of white space down the page from the begin statement to the end statement. This makes it clear where each structure starts and finishes, and which structures are nested in others. Some languages, such as Python, actually use the indentation as part of the rules of the language. However, in most languages, it is down to the programmer to get this right.

Limiting the length of a line of code to about 80 characters will ensure that the indentation is preserved when a hard copy of the code is printed.

Formatting

As well as the vertical white spaces created by indentation, the code should be grouped into logical blocks that perform parts of the main task by entering blank lines between them. This is the equivalent of writing a piece of text in paragraphs which each focus on one aspect of the whole story.

Commenting

Most languages provide the facility to insert **comments** in the code that are read by the programmer but ignored by the computer. These comments are vital to making the code understandable and should be written while the code is written and not after the code has been written.

There are several instances where comments should be included in the code:

- There should be a program header comment at the beginning of the code. This comment will include the name of the program, what the program does, the names of the programmers, the date of the last update and notes on what is currently being worked on or any known and unresolved bugs.
- Each subroutine should have a comment at the beginning explaining what the subroutine does and how it will be called, including any parameters that are necessary to call the subroutine.
- Where variables and constants are declared, a short comment should be given explaining their purpose.
- The code itself should have inline comments explaining the algorithm. These comments should come before the code they refer to. There should be enough comments to explain the entire algorithm. In other words, if the code was deleted and the comments left, it should be possible for another programmer to use the comments to produce code that works in the same way.

This last point does not imply that every line of code should be commented. Consider the following commented code that opens a patient file and retrieves the notes entered on a given date:

```
// Read PatientID
INPUT PatientID
// Read Date
INPUT GivenDate
// Open Patient File for Input
```

```
OPEN File "PatientID.txt" for Input
// Set the Found flag to false
Found = False
// Start a loop
REPEAT
  //Read an entry from file
  Read PatientNotesEntry
  //Check if this is the correct entry
  IF PatientNotesEntry.Date = GivenDate THEN
    //Print the details from that date
    PRINT PatientNotesEntry.Comment
    //Set the Found flag to TRUE
    Found = True
  //end the if statement
  END IF
//Carry on looping until the end of the file or
//record has been found.
UNTIL end_of_file or Found = True
```

The comments are obviously far too excessive and get in the way of making the code understandable. Many of the comments just simply repeat what the code is saying without adding any extra meaning. A more useful way to comment this program is as follows:

```
// Read PatientID and date
INPUT PatientID
INPUT GivenDate

// Open Patient File
OPEN File "PatientID.txt" for Input

// Initialise flag to false
Found = False

// Loop through reading one item from the file at a time until
// the desired date is found, or the end of the file is reached
REPEAT

Read PatientNotesEntry

  //If the item read matches the date, print comment and set
    //found flag
  IF PatientNotesEntry.Date = GivenDate THEN
    PRINT PatientNotesEntry.Comment
    Found = True
  END IF

UNTIL end_of_file or Found = True
```

The comments in this second example are more useful in explaining the program, and despite the fact that there isn't one comment for every line of code, the comments still explain the whole algorithm.

END OF CHAPTER QUESTIONS

1 Here is an extract from the algorithm for a program that calculates and prints the bill in a youth hostel:

```
01 Const Room_Rate = 5.25
02 DIM Total AS Currency
03
04 PROCEDURE CalculateTotal
05    DIM Nights as Integer
06    Input Nights
07    Total = Nights * Room_Rate
08 END PROCEDURE
09
10 BEGIN Main Program
11    Print Bill_Header
12    CalculateTotal
13    Print "Amount to pay :", Total
14 END Main Program
```

(a) From the extract of code above, state an identifier that has been used for:
   (i)   a constant
   (ii) a global variable
   (iii) a local variable
   (iv) a subroutine. (4)

(b) Explain **one** advantage of using a constant in the algorithm above. (2)

(c) The hostel request that the number of nights should also be shown on the bill. A programmer attempts to do this by changing line 13 as follows:

```
13    PRINT "Total to Pay for ", Nights, "Nights :", Total
```

   (i) State why this new version of line 13 will not work. (1)
   (ii) Describe how the program can be altered so that the number of nights is correctly printed. (2)

2 Name and describe **two** techniques that can be used when writing a program in a high level language to help with program maintenance. (6)

[OCR AS Computing paper 2506 – June 2006]

3 A portable mp3 player stores the lengths of songs (in seconds) in a one-dimensional array called TrackLength(). The array contains 100 integers. If there are fewer than 100 songs then the array uses as many elements as it needs, starting from TrackLength(1). The remaining elements are set to 0.

For example, if there are 16 songs, their lengths will be stored in TrackLength(1) to TrackLength(16). TrackLength(17) to TrackLength(100) will be set to 0.

Write code in a high level language to calculate the total length of the songs stored in minutes and seconds. You should state the name of the language you are using, and use good program writing techniques to make your code easy to understand and maintain.

4 Discuss why it is necessary for programmers to use good program writing techniques and coding style when writing code. You should refer to specific techniques and how they benefit the programmer.

The quality of your written communication will be assessed in your answer to this question. (6)

Chapter 12 Testing and Running a Solution

In this chapter we discuss the three main types of error that occur when you are writing a computer program and how they are detected and resolved. This includes techniques and strategies for testing programs. We will discuss the tools available in programming languages to help you find and eliminate errors in your code.

Program code needs to be **translated** so that the computer can understand it and execute it. Also, the program may be used on a different computer from the computer on which it was written, so it must be transferred onto the target computer, a process known as **installation**. We will discuss the processes of translation and installation.

1. Types of programming error

The errors a programmer will make while writing a program fall under three categories depending on the point at which the error occurs, and how they can be noticed:

- **Syntax Error**: this is an error that occurs when a statement has been written in the program that breaks the rules of that programming language. This means that the statement cannot be understood by the computer, and cannot be executed.
- **Logic Error**: this is an error that occurs because there is a mistake in the algorithm that results in the program doing something other than what it was intended to do.
- **Run-time Error**: this is an error which occurs due to an unexpected situation with the data being processed or another external factor. The program would otherwise work under normal operating conditions.

We shall look at each of these errors in turn. For this we shall use a program that reads a file of integers, and outputs the mean of these integers. An algorithm for this program would be:

```
01   BEGIN
02     Total = 0
03     Count = 0
04     OPEN File For Input
05     WHILE NOT End Of File
06       Read Number from File
07       Total = Total + Number
08       Count = Count + 1
09     END WHILE
10     CLOSE File
11     OUTPUT Total / Count
12   END
```

Syntax errors

If the programmer writes line 07 as:

Total + Number = Total

The computer will not be able to execute that statement. This is because the rule for writing an assignment statement (in most languages) requires the left-hand side to be a single variable. This is a common **syntax error** made by students who are learning programming for the first time.

Before executing any statement, it has to be translated. This means that the high-level code in which the program is written is converted to low-level machine code that the computer can execute. When translating the statement, the computer compares it with the formats of statements that are allowed in the rules of the language. But a statement with a syntax error will not fit any pattern and so cannot be translated. As a result, the computer will not understand the instruction and will produce an error message during the translation.

Other common causes of syntax errors are:

- missing/extra punctuation or brackets separating parts of a statement
- not using enough arguments for functions or procedures
- missing part of a multi-line statement (such as IF without END IF, or FOR without NEXT, etc.)
- using unrecognised identifiers in languages where all identifiers have to be declared
- type mismatch – when the computer expects data of a certain data type, but the data provided is of a different type.

Misspelling words in the code will also often generate a syntax error, especially if you misspell a keyword. This will usually be because it will create an unrecognised identifier. On the very slight chance that the misspelt word is actually an identifier recognised by the computer, then it is most likely that it will have been used incorrectly according to the rules of the language.

An interesting situation would occur if line 08 of the mean algorithm was written as:

Count = Count = 1

In languages where the = is used both for assignment and comparison, this is likely to be interpreted by the computer as:

Count = (Count = 1) or "Count becomes (count is the same as 1)"

If the computer expects Count to be an integer, then it will produce a syntax error because there is a type mismatch. Count is an integer, while (Count = 1) evaluates to a Boolean. Enforcing strict use of the correct data type like this is called **strong typing**. Not all languages are strongly typed. Some languages will automatically convert data to an appropriate data type. In this example, it will convert the Boolean (Count =1) to an integer such as 0 or -1. This will not produce a syntax error, but a logic error.

The solution to a syntax error is to correct the syntax in the statements where there is an error. The translator will usually help by indicating where the error is likely to be and what has caused it. This is called **translator diagnostics**. Some translators may even suggest corrections. Note that the translator's diagnostics and suggested solutions are not necessarily right and the programmer should check the syntax carefully. Most programming languages have online or paper-based reference material that explains what the correct syntax is.

Logic errors

If all the statements in the program can be understood and translated by the computer, then any errors still in the program will most likely be **logic errors**.

One common source of logic errors is incorrect mathematical formulae. For example, in the mean algorithm, if instead of writing:

OUTPUT Total / Count

the programmer writes:

OUTPUT Count / Total

the computer will understand this instruction and run, but will produce an incorrect result.

Logic errors usually do not produce error messages and are only discovered because the computer is producing unexpected results.

Other common causes for logic errors are:

- instructions in the wrong order
- incorrect conditions for IF statements or Loops.

Run-time errors

When the syntax (how the instructions are written) and the logic (what the instructions do) are both correct, the program should work under normal circumstances. However, in some extreme circumstances, the code will require a computer to perform an impossible operation that will cause it to crash or to stop responding. All such errors are called **run-time errors**.

For example, the mean algorithm works correctly in most cases. However, if the file of numbers happens to be empty, then Total will be 0, and Count will be 0. So, line 11 will attempt to output 0 divided by 0. Because division by 0 is an impossible arithmetic operation, the program will crash. Other arithmetic operations that will cause an error include calculating the square root of a negative number. Run-time errors like this, which are due to the

> Note: The 'logic of a program' refers to the instructions in the program and the order in which they are executed. A logic error is therefore an error in writing down what the program does.

computer attempting an impossible arithmetic operation, are called **arithmetic errors**.

A different type of run-time error would occur in the mean algorithm if the file from which the numbers are to be read had been deleted. The computer would not be able to carry out line 04 because the file is not found, and will crash with an error message.

Other common causes of run-time errors are:

- Overflow error – when the program attempts to use a variable to store a value that is too large for it. (For example, storing 4500 x 1000) in a two byte integer which can only store integers between -32768 and 32767).
- Stack overflow error – when the program runs out of stack space to store the operations of the program. This can happen especially when the program is executing a recursive algorithm.
- Library error – the program refers to an external library that does not exist, or incorrectly refers to functions in an external library.

In order to prevent run-time errors, the program has to be written such that every extreme situation which can be anticipated has been taken into account and steps have been taken to ensure that it will not crash the program. This is called making the program **robust**.

If an error condition can be detected, additional code should be written so that instead of crashing, the program will produce an error message and close in an acceptable way. For example, in our program to calculate the average of numbers in a file, the program should first check whether the file exists before attempting to open it. If the file does not exist, the program should output an error message to the user explaining why the operation cannot continue.

A very common reason why arithmetic errors occur is that calculations are being performed by the computer on incorrect data that have been input by the user. Therefore every input from the user should be validated to ensure that only inputs that will produce sensible results are accepted.

Some programming languages also offer **exception-handling** (or **error-handling**) facilities. This means you can write code telling the computer what to do if a run-time error occurs in the program.

2. Testing strategies

Testing refers to all the ways in which the programmer ensures that there are no errors in the program.

Testing should be carried out throughout the development of the program, although the nature of the testing will be different at each stage.

It is important to have a carefully defined **test strategy**. The test strategy specifies what type of testing should be carried out at each stage.

We shall look at different ways of testing.

Black box testing

Black box testing techniques are only concerned with the inputs and the outputs of the program, and not how the program works. You are testing whether the inputs produce the output that would be expected.

Ideally when completing a black box test, you would test every possible input to the program, and if each input produces the right output then you can be satisfied that the program would work in all cases. However, testing all possible inputs is impossible in all but the most trivial programs. Therefore, it is necessary to group the inputs into groups that are similar and test a representative value for each group. If the test for that representative value is successful, then we assume that all other values in that group have been tested.

You also need to make sure that you have considered all kinds of input data:

- **Valid data:** data which you would normally expect the user to input.
- **Invalid data:** data which should generate an error message if it was input.
- **Borderline data:** you need to be especially careful to test the data at the boundaries between different cases, to ensure that they are dealt with correctly.

< Example >

The maximum length of a single text message (or SMS) in Unicode (16-bit characters) is 70 characters. If a text message is too long, it is split into smaller messages that are sent separately. A mobile phone manufacturer is writing software that splits the message entered by the user into the correct number of text messages. They have decided that their phones will not send blank messages.

Produce a set of black box test data to test this software. For each test case, give the test data, the reason for the test, the kind of test data that it is and the expected outcome.

Solution:

Test data	Reason for test	Kind of test data	Expected outcome
"" (Empty text message)	Message of length 0	Invalid data	Error message "Blank SMS"
" AAAAAAAAAABBBBBBBBBB "	Message of length between 1 and 69	Valid data	Message sent whole as 1 SMS
"AAAAAAAAAABBBBBBBBBB AAAAAAAAAABBBBBBBBBB AAAAAAAAAABBBBBBBBBB AAAAAAAAAABBBBBBBBBB AAAAAAAAAABBBBBBBBBB AAAAAAAAAABBBBBBBBBB AAAAAAAAAABBBBBBBBBB"	Message of length exactly 70	Borderline data	Message sent whole as 1 SMS
" AAAAAAAAAABBBBBBBBBB AAAAAAAAAABBBBBBBBBB AAAAAAAAAABBBBBBBBBB AAAAAAAAAABBBBBBBBBB AAAAAAAAAABBBBBBBBBB AAAAAAAAAABBBBBBBBBB AAAAAAAAAABBBBBBBBBB AAAAAAAAAABBBBBBBBBB"	Message of length greater than 70	Valid data	Message split into 2 SMSs and sent

Notice the reason for test describes the category in which the test data falls. By testing the message "AAAAAAAAAABBBBBBBBBB" we have implicitly tested all messages that have a length between 1 and 69 characters. Testing another message such as "Hello Mum" would not be a new test case, but just another example for the test case given. It is not significantly different from "AAAAAAAAAABBBBBBBBBB" within the context of what we are testing.

White box testing techniques

Unlike black box testing, which is mainly concerned with the inputs and the outputs of the program, **white box testing** techniques test the algorithm in the code to make sure that all parts of the algorithm function as intended. The focus is therefore on identifying and testing every possible route or path of execution through the program.

On each test run, the path of execution is noted, so that it can be compared with other runs. This path consists of the numbers of the lines of code that are executed. The path of execution is determined by the values of the conditions in constructs such as IF statements and condition-controlled loops. It is therefore useful to also note whether the condition was TRUE or FALSE during the execution.

< Example >

The following algorithm inputs a year as an integer and outputs whether or not it is a leap year:

```
01   BEGIN
02   INPUT Year
03   IF Year is not an integer greater than
     0 THEN
04    OUTPUT "Invalid input"
05   ELSE
06    IF Year is divisible by 100 THEN
07     IF Year is divisible by 400 THEN
08      OUTPUT "LEAP YEAR"
09     ELSE
10      OUTPUT "NOT A LEAP YEAR"
11     END IF
12    ELSE
13     IF Year is divisible by 4 then
14      OUTPUT "LEAP YEAR"
15     ELSE
16      OUTPUT "NOT A LEAP YEAR"
17     END IF
18    END IF
19   END IF
20   END {OF ALGORITHM}
```

Perform a white box test on this algorithm by selecting appropriate test data and for each test data, list the path of execution through the algorithm and the output. For every line with an IF statement, indicate in the path whether the value of the condition is TRUE or FALSE.

SOLUTION

First we consider a year like 2000.

Input Data: 2000
Path of Execution: 01, 02, 03(FALSE), 05, 06(TRUE), 07(TRUE), 08, 11, 18, 19 and 20
Output: LEAP YEAR

When choosing subsequent test data we are aiming to choose data that will go through a different path. We'll try the string "nanana".

Input Data: nanana
Path of Execution: 01, 02, 03(TRUE), 04, 19 and 20
Output: INVALID INPUT

For the third test case we try the data 2009.

Input Data: 2009
Path of Execution: 01, 02, 03(FALSE), 05, 06(FALSE), 12, 13(FALSE), 15, 16, 17, 18, 19 and 20
Output: NOT A LEAP YEAR

< Activity >

There are two more test cases which lead through different paths of execution. Can you find them?

Alpha and beta testing

Alpha and beta testing are carried out when the software is nearly complete and is being tested as a whole. They apply especially to commercial software that is being developed by a software company for an external end user. The difference between alpha and beta testing resides in the stage in which it takes place and who performs the testing.

Alpha testing takes place within the company producing the software and employees of the company test the program as though they were potential users. At this stage, the software is not complete and there will be several bugs that the company is aware of and resolving. Restricting the testing to a small number of people within the company allows the company to easily replace the version being tested with the latest version as soon as bugs are fixed. (They also do not run the risk of being sued by a third party for supplying faulty software that may damage their computer or their data).

Beta testing takes place after the alpha testing is complete and any faults that were discovered have been resolved. The software is by now very similar to the final product. It is released to potential users outside the company who test the software in the actual conditions in which it is intended to be used. This is useful, as end users may find bugs that the company had not anticipated. The beta testers also send constructive comments about the features of the program that the company can use to improve the software.

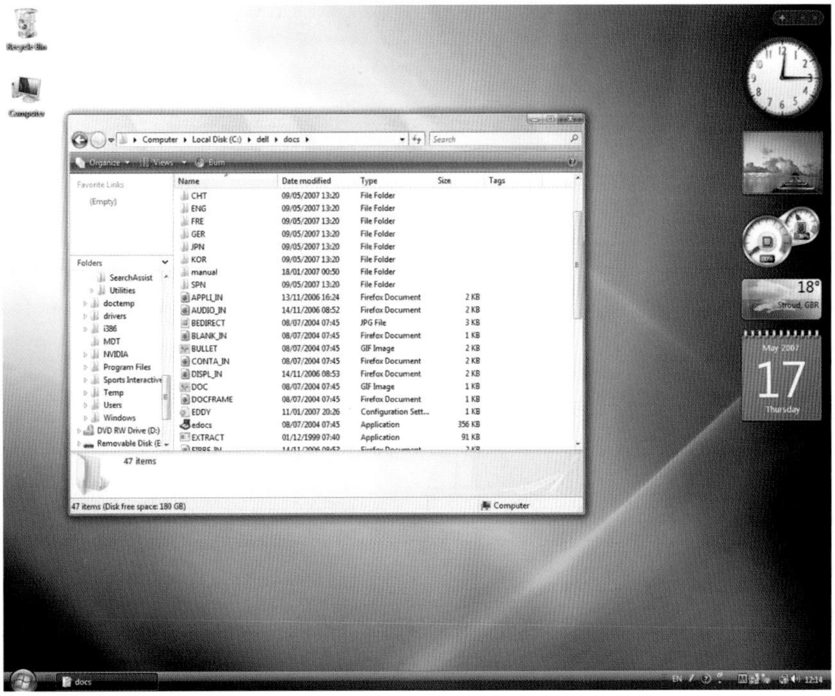

Figure 2.17 Microsoft's operating system Windows Vista was beta tested for 18 months from July 2005 to its release in January 2007

Acceptance testing

While the purpose of most testing is to find and eliminate bugs and errors in the software, the purpose of **acceptance testing** is to demonstrate to the end user that the software works correctly and all desired features have been implemented.

Acceptance testing therefore takes place after all other development and testing of the software is complete and the software is ready to be handed to the end user.

The software is tested against all the requirements agreed between the developers and the end user before development started.

3. Debugging tools

Most programming languages provide facilities for finding and removing the faults or bugs in software. These are called **debugging tools**.

The most obvious is **translator diagnostics**. These are messages generated by the translator, while it is translating the source code into object code. As we have seen earlier, this is useful for finding out where there are syntax errors in the code. However, they can include more than just syntax errors. They often include warnings where there might be a logic error, for example, if a variable is declared but never used.

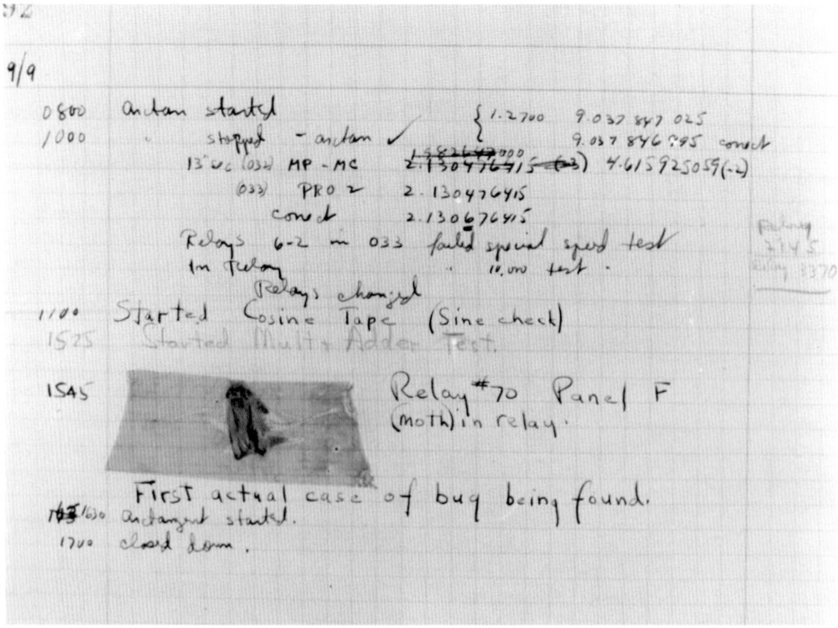

Figure 2.18 The first ever computer bug?

To find a logic error, it is useful to be able to watch the program in operation. This can be achieved using **breakpoints** and **stepping**. A breakpoint is a marker added to a line of code requesting that the program stop running when it gets to that line. At this point, the programmer can cause the program to run one instruction or step at a time. This is called stepping. It allows the programmer to check the actual logic of the program against what it is expected to do.

Breakpoints are also useful for carrying out **variable checks**. When the execution has stopped, the programmer can request the values of variables that are used in the program and compare them against the values that would be expected to verify that the program is working up to this point. Some languages even allow you to set breakpoints which stop the program running whenever the value of a variable changes, rather than on a specific line.

Dry runs

Sometimes, in order to locate the cause and location of an error, it is useful to go through the code manually, executing and recording each line in turn as if you were the programmer. This is called a **dry run**.

A dry run is often carried out using a trace table, which gives us a systematic way of recording what happens when the section of code is executed. The trace table has a column for the line of code being executed, a column for every variable used, and a column for recording any values that are output. (A column can also be included for comments). As the programmer goes through the code manually, a new line is added to the table for each line executed. On each new line, any changes to the values of the variable or the outputs are recorded. Alternatively, several lines of code can be recorded on one line of the trace table, as long as the order in which the variables are changed is clear.

Note: This is one of the oldest algorithms known. It was described by the Greek Mathematician Euclid around 300BC and was referred to by some writers before him.

< Example >

Here is an algorithm which calculates the highest common factor of two integers. Trace the algorithm when the inputs are 24 and 30.

```
01    INPUT X, Y
02    WHILE X > 0
03      N = X
04      X = Y Mod X
05      Y = N
06    END WHILE
07    OUTPUT Y
```

Solution:

The first step is to determine the variables in the algorithm. These are N, X and Y. The trace table can then be drawn and completed as follows:

Lines	N	X	Y	OUTPUT	Comment
01 INPUT X,Y		24	30		
02 WHILE X > 0					TRUE, so go to line 03
03 N = X	24				
04 X = Y MOD X		6			
05 Y = N			24		
06 END WHILE					Return to line 03
03 WHILE X > 0					TRUE, so go to line 03 again
03 N = X	6				
04 X = Y MOD X		0			
05 Y = N			6		
06 END WHILE					Return to line 03
03 WHILE X > 0					False so go to line 07
07 OUTPUT Y				6	

< Activity >

Carry out dry runs for the same algorithm, using different sets of input. You may use the trace table as provided, or alternatively, you may choose to group some lines of code together (e.g. lines 03, 04 and 05).

4. Installation and execution

In this Unit you have been writing programs in a high-level language with instructions that are to be executed by the computer. The code you have written is referred to as **source code**. It cannot be executed directly by the computer unless it is translated by a translator program into **object code** that the computer can understand and execute.

When software is being developed and tested, this is usually done on the programmer's computer. This computer typically has the translator program that converts the high-level source code that the program is written in, to object code that is executed by the computer. It also has its files organised in a particular way, and may have some external libraries already installed which are used in the software.

It is necessary to ensure that the finished version will run smoothly on the end user's computer, although it may be set up differently from the programmer's computer. This is called **installing** the program on the end user's computer.

Many programming languages allow the programmer to translate the program and produce a file containing the object code that can be executed on its own, without the source code. This makes providing the program to the end user easier; they can be given the object code as an executable file that will run on its own. In this case, the program can be installed manually – the necessary files are just copied to a convenient location on the end user's computer. If an executable file is not available, then the source code and the translator program need to be copied to the end user's computer.

Sometimes, having just the executable code (or the source code and translator program) is not enough to allow the end user to run the program, because of other files the program depends on.

In this case we need an installation routine. This is a program that will automate the installation process. The installation routine is usually delivered with the software on removable media such as a CD-ROM or over the Internet.

Some of the functions carried out by the installation routine are:

- Copy the executable program (or the source code and translator) to the correct folder on the end user's computer.
- Copy or prepare any data files that are needed by the program, ensuring that they are in the correct folder, where the program will expect them.
- Copy any library files that the program uses and register them on the end user's computer if necessary.
- Make the program easy to access by setting up icons, menu buttons or shortcuts for the convenience of the end user.
- Initial configuration of user preference settings in the program (e.g. options like language or colour scheme).

Some programming languages provide facilities for creating installation routines as well as executable files of the software that has been written.

END OF CHAPTER QUESTIONS

1   A program has been written which is intended to accept the ages of the five members of a secondary school chess team and to output the average (mean) age. Each age is input in digits as a whole number of years.
State **three** different sets of test data that could be used as part of a test plan to test this program, giving a reason for each set of data.   (6)

[OCR AS Computing paper 2506 – June 2006]

2   Describe **three** methods or tools that can be used to identify programming errors.   (6)

[OCR AS Computing paper 2506 – June 2006]

3   Explain what is meant by the following types of programming error and give an example of each:
    (i)   syntax Error
    (ii)   logic Error
    (iii) arithmetic Error.   (6)

[OCR AS Computing paper 2506 – June 2006]

4 (a) State what is meant by:
       (i)   white box testing
       (ii) black box testing.   (2)

   (b) The following function outputs the maximum of its three parameters A, B and C:

```
01  Function Maximum(A,B,C)
02   If A >= B THEN
03   IF C >= A THEN
04      RETURN C
05    ELSE
06      RETURN A
07    END IF
08    ELSE
09    IF C >= B THEN
10      RETURN C
11    ELSE
12      RETURN B
13    END IF
14   END IF
15  END FUNCTION

When the function is called with Maximum(3,4,1) the path of
execution, showing the results of IF statements, is:

01, 02 (FALSE), 08, 09(FALSE), 11, 12, 13, 14, 15.
```

   The value returned is 4.

   State **two** more input data that will lead to a different path of execution, and for each, list the path of
   execution in the same format as above, and state the value returned.   (8)

5 Many programs are bought on CD-ROM and need to be installed onto a computer before they can
   be used.

   Discuss why it is necessary to install the program and what happens during installation.

   The quality of your written communication will be assessed in your answer to this question.   (6)

Chapter 13 The Function of Operating Systems

1. Features of operating systems

The operating system (OS) must:

- provide and manage hardware resources such as the management of memory and the jobs passing through it
- provide an interface between the user and the machine, which we discussed in Chapter 2.4
- provide an interface between applications software and the machine. This is not so obvious as a user interface, but here there are two disparate things; software and hardware. Something needs to ensure that the instructions which make up the software and the hardware which has to be used to interpret the instructions and make them do something useful can communicate with each other
- provide security for the data on the system particularly when there are a number of users who have access to the system
- provide utility software to allow maintenance to be done.

2. Interrupt handling

The normal functioning of a computer processor is serial in nature. An instruction is collected, it is acted upon and then the next instruction is fetched. This continues while the processor is operating or until the set of program instructions is completed. During this time there are all sorts of things that can happen which will mean that the processor should stop what it is doing and do something else instead. Typical things that might crop up are that the buffer that is being used to transmit data from primary memory to secondary storage has been emptied and is requesting to be refilled in order that data transfer can continue (as described in Chapter 4.2). For this to happen, the processor must stop what it is doing and transfer the data. It is the **interrupt** that asks for this to happen. There are various types of interrupt, ranging from hardware interrupts, of which the buffer is an example, to software interrupts such as an interrupt caused to the flow of a program by a call to an external device. Each of the interrupts is given a priority because if two occur at the same time it is important to know which is most important. The most important type of interrupt is the one that might happen if there is an interruption in power supply (this is given the highest priority of all). It is important to understand the process that happens when an interrupt occurs.

To begin with, the interrupt itself is stored with all the other jobs that the processor has to do, including the one that it is currently running. Each interrupt is given a priority, as is the current job, according to how important it is. All these jobs are not just stored but they are stored in order of priority. Each time the processor finishes an instruction it checks the list of jobs that still have to be done. As long as the job it is doing is at the top of the list it will carry on and do the next instruction, but if something like an interrupt has come in which has gone to the top of the list because it is important, then the processor must stop the job that it is doing. It can't just stop because it would have wasted the processing it has done already. It has to store the contents of all the special registers, which we studied in Chapter 4.1, so that when it goes back to the job it can load the special registers with these contents again and carry on from where it left off. These values are stored in a stack that we will return to in Chapter 17. When this has been done the new job, which is our interrupt, can be loaded into the special registers and processed until it is carried out or until something even more important enters the list of jobs to do – in which case the whole process is gone through again.

< Activity >

Find out about the different types of interrupts that can occur.

Remember to return here when the type of storage that is used for the storage of the contents of the special registers is explained in Chapter 17. This type of storage is called a **stack**.

One thing that remains unexplained is the method used by the computer to understand what it is that an interrupt is asking to be done and how it can do it. One answer is the use of vectored interrupts that are not part of our course but may be an interesting starting point for further study.

3. Scheduling, job queues and priorities

In Chapter 2.3 we met the idea that the computer could be made to work in different ways according to the type of operating system that is used. Many of those operating systems have in common the fact that in order to work there must be a number of jobs in the computer's memory at the same time. If, for instance, the operating system is a multi-tasking operating system there are a number of jobs that must be in the memory in order for the OS to switch from one job to another. This, in turn, means that the OS must have a set of rules that it can use in order to determine the order in which the jobs should be handled. The use of this set of rules is known as job **scheduling**.

The rules used will be largely decided by the importance applied to the different jobs to be carried out. This concept of 'importance' implies that the jobs can be arranged into some sort of order and the OS can then follow this order of jobs. The question arises, 'How is the order of jobs decided?'

< Discuss >

Why are I/O jobs given a higher priority than processor-bound jobs?

One way of ordering jobs is to divide jobs into those jobs that are going to use printers and other peripherals a lot, such as a job to print gas bills, etc. and jobs that use the processor a lot, such as a program to calculate the 3 millionth prime number. The big difference here is the proportion of time that the processor spends communicating with the outside world. The two types of job mentioned here are called **I/O bound jobs** and **processor-bound jobs**.

This simple priority is a scheduling algorithm. Some other scheduling algorithms are:

- FCFS, which stands for 'first come first served'
- RR or round robin – the concept of every user getting a small amount of time with the processor before it goes on to the next user. We met this in Chapter 3 when discussing multi-access OSs. It uses time slices of various lengths to ensure that all jobs get a share of processor time
- SJF, which stands for shortest job first. When new jobs are added it is important to make sure they are placed in the right place in the queue by the OS making an estimate of the length of time required to carry out the task
- SRT, or shortest remaining time is similar to SJF except that jobs will obviously get shorter and hence nearer the top of the queue as they are processed. Jobs are returned to the queue when they have to stop for some reason like waiting for some input from a keyboard. The major problem with this scheduling algorithm is that longer jobs may never get started
- MFQ or multi-level feedback queues. This is a very complex algorithm involving a number of queues set up according to original rules and acting very like a set of league tables. As jobs are given a long amount of processor time without finishing, or when they require long periods of peripheral time, they will drop down the league tables, sometimes getting relegated. When a job is relegated or is finished and leaves the system, another job can be promoted. In this way jobs are not allowed to spend too much time monopolising the processor.

Scheduling is used in order to try to maximise the use of the computer and all its peripherals. It should do this while being 'fair' to all the users and ensuring that there is a reasonable response time for all. Finally, it should ensure that above all the algorithm is robust so that the system will not fail either through overloading or by becoming blocked.

In order to understand the ability of a computer to have a number of jobs being in different stages of processing at a time it is important to know the way that a processor treats jobs.

Any job is in one of three states: ready, running or blocked:

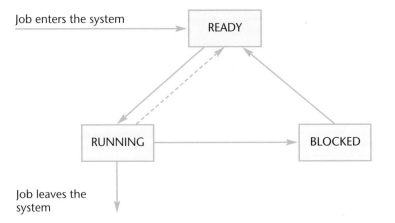

Figure 3.1

The part of the OS that controls jobs around the processor is called the **scheduler**. There are a number of tasks that have to be done and they are carried out by different parts of the scheduler. When a job wants to be processed it must enter the system and be placed in a queue of jobs waiting for processing, called the **ready queue**. The part of the scheduler that loads the job into the ready queue is called the **High Level Scheduler** (HLS). When the job that is currently running has had to stop then the job at the top of the ready queue is loaded into the processor and is run. This is done by the **Low Level Scheduler** (LLS). Jobs may leave the running state for one of three reasons:

■ the job may have finished running in which case it will leave the system
■ the job may require the services of a peripheral, for instance it may need some printing to be carried out, in which case it will stop running and be placed in the blocked queue to await servicing. When the job is ready to start running again it has to go back to the ready queue and wait there for its turn
■ the job has had long enough and it has to give up its place so that the other jobs get a chance. There have to be rules for this to happen, an obvious one being in a multi-access system where each user gets a time slice. When the time slice has ended, the job has to be returned to the ready queue to wait for its next turn.

Another reason for a job being stopped from running and having to give up the processor time is if a higher priority interrupt comes along.

We have seen how part of the scheduler is called the HLS and part is the LLS. There is a third part called the **Medium Level Scheduler**, which controls the movement of jobs between the primary memory and the secondary storage.

The scheduler that has been described here is called a **pre-emptive scheduler** because it is allowed to move jobs out of the running state and into the **ready queue** (the dotted arrow in Figure 3.1 on page 136). If the job that is in the running state can only be moved out of it because it has finished processing or because it needs some I/O then that dotted arrow can be completely removed and the scheduler is said to be non-pre-emptive.

In reality the ready queue is likely to be a number of queues, each holding jobs of different priorities, so the jobs from queue 2 will not be allowed into the running state before queue 1 is emptied.

4. Memory management

What does memory actually look like? We now have an idea that it contains the OS and a number of jobs.

Primary Memory

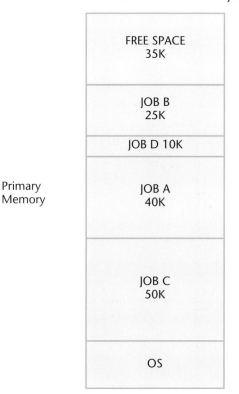

Figure 3.2

The diagram above shows the state of memory if it contains Jobs A, B, C and D to be processed, and the OS. Imagine that the maximum size of the memory available to the jobs is 160k. The four jobs that are there have been loaded by the MLS. Now, imagine that the job with the next highest priority is Job E and that it is of size 40k. There is only 35k of free space so the job will have to wait. The various jobs now take their turn in the running state until one of them leaves the system. Its space in the memory can be used for something else. If the job that finished is Job C there is no problem because there will be ample space. If it is Job B that finishes there is still no problem because there is now plenty of space when B's space is added to the free space above it. But what happens if the job to finish is Job D? One of a number of courses of action could be followed:

1. neither of the 'gaps' is big enough so we wait until a gap appears that is big enough
2. part of Job E is put in the free space area and the rest is put in where Job D used to be, leaving some of that space as the free space
3. Job B could be moved down to Job A, which would have the effect of making the free space big enough for Job E.

Option 1 seems to be a waste of resources and what would happen if the next job were greater than 160k anyway?

Option 2 splits up the job, but more importantly splits up memory in an unpredictable way. If you can imagine this, after the system has been running for a few hundred jobs the memory will be split into smaller and smaller areas, and it will become fragmented and the effect will be to adversely affect the performance.

Option 3 seems the best option and is easy if you are just looking at moving areas around on a diagram, but remember that these jobs are programs. In these programs each instruction has references to set up memory locations and moving a job means that all of these have to be recalculated.

One solution to this problem is that memory can be split up into small sections called **pages**. These pages are all the same size; let's imagine 5k in our example, and each job uses a number of the pages. As long as an index is kept to show where all the jobs are, then dividing jobs up will not cause a problem.

PRIMARY MEMORY

FREE SPACE

JOB B

JOB D

JOB A

JOB C

O.S.

	Index	
Page	Page	Content
1	1	FS1
2	2	FS2
3	3	FS3
4	'	
5	'	
6	'	
7	7	FS7
8	8	B1
9	'	
10	'	
11	'	
12	12	B5
13	13	D1
14	'	
15	'	
16	'	
17	'	
18	'	
19	'	
20	'	
21	'	
22	'	
23	'	
24	'	
25	'	
26	'	
27	'	
28	'	
29	'	
30	30	C8
31	31	C9
32	32	C10

Figure 3.3

< Discuss >

This system seems very straightforward. The OS has only to look at the index to find out where the next page of a particular job is. However, there is still a problem of keeping track of addresses. Discuss how this problem might be solved.

Figure 3.4

When Job D leaves the system, Job E (needs 8 pages) can be inserted.

Index

Page	Page	Content
1	1	E1
2	2	E2
3	3	E3
4	4	E4
5	5	E5
6	6	E6
7	7	E7
8	8	B1
9	9	B2
10	10	B3
11	11	B4
12	12	B5
13	13	E8
14	14	FS1
15	15	A1
16	16	A2

JOB E

Primary Memory
(Job D Out
Job E In)

JOB B

JOB E

FREE SPACE

If the memory is too small to hold a particular job or it is necessary to store more jobs in the memory simultaneously then the OS can make use of the fact that whatever job is being processed at the moment, only one page of that job can be worked on at a time. Consequently, what is the point in having the whole job present at the same time? Why not only store that page? When it becomes necessary to move to another page then the required page can be loaded into the memory and the previous page can be dispensed with. If the OS can predict the next page that will be needed it can get that page ready to be input to the memory by moving it into a special type of storage called **virtual memory**. Virtual memory is not part of primary memory but it does behave in a similar way and provides high-speed input to the memory.

A problem can arise with moving pages in and out of memory, even if virtual memory is used, when the code has many jump instructions. Imagine the extreme case where a jump sends the processor to another page of the code. This code is input via virtual memory and it overwrites the original page. This new page immediately has a branch instruction back to the original page. This original page needs to be found and imported into the memory, where it will probably overwrite the page that has only just been put in memory. If this now happens again we have the ridiculous situation of the processor spending more time moving pages in and out of the memory than it spends doing the processing. This situation is called **disk thrashing** because it involves the disk continually being searched for pages.

< Discuss >

How can the OS keep track of addresses when segmentation of memory is used?

When a new segment is called into memory that is larger than the previous segment how can the segment be placed (as it needs to overwrite more than it is entitled to)?

Splitting the memory and the jobs into pages of equal size makes things fairly straightforward to control because the indexing system can keep track of everything. However, it is not a very sensible way to split up pieces of code. Far more sensible would be to have a procedure in a page and then another page for the next procedure, and so on. The problem is that if the procedures are smaller than a page then space is wasted and if they are larger than a page then more than one page is required and we are back to having arbitrary dividing lines. Why not allow the pages to vary in size? These divisions are more sensible because they follow logical splits in code and data but the control is very much more complex because the system can no longer predict the beginning and end of a section. When the code is split like this the areas of memory inhabited and indexed are known as **segments**.

Note that segmentation means dividing up memory space on logical lines while paging is dividing memory up on physical lines.

5. Spooling

If a job requires printout then there could be a sizable delay in carrying on with the processing of the job because the processor has to send data to the printer for printing out. The printer is relatively slow at carrying out its task, causing there to be a speed mismatch between the processor and the printer. We mentioned this problem and a solution to it using buffers and interrupts in Chapter 4. However, imagine the print job is going to take a lot of time, requiring multiple downloads to the printer, or that the printer is already busy printing out a different job – the result will be a slowing down of the processor. This effect is easy to see in a classroom at the end of a lesson when everyone wants a printout and there are a limited number of printers. The solution is to store all the print jobs on the secondary storage device and then to print them from the disk so that the processor(s) can get on with something else. It would be unfair to just take them at random, so it seems reasonable to take them in the order that they arrived. This implies that the system will need to store them in a queue. It would be difficult to do this because they are all of different sizes and if the queue is going to be stored in a standard data structure, like an array, then the items need to be of a standard size. For this reason the jobs themselves, which are all going to be of different sizes, are simply stored randomly on the storage device (probably a hard disk). In order to be able to find them again, the system stores references to the jobs and their location in a queue. It is this queue that is called the **spool queue**.

In addition to this, it may arise that a print job needs to be done before jobs that have already arrived because it has a high priority. This means that the details of this job need to be placed in the queue or at the front of the queue rather than at the end.

< Activity >

Not only is the spool queue not a queue of jobs, it is not really a queue at all, because a queue only allows jobs to enter at one end. After you have studied Chapter 17 of the specification come back here and try to work out what the spooling system actually looks like.

6. Modern personal computer operating systems

When the computer is switched on it can only use the data that is in the ROM, and generally this will be a small instruction set. It starts by running the POST (power on self test), which basically allows it to check that all the parts that it needs to 'come to life' are there and available. It clears anything that may still be in the registers in the CPU and then loads the address of the first instruction in the boot program into the program counter. Control is now passed to the boot program that carries out its own checks on the hardware and if any BIOS is found, probably on the hard disk or on a storage device called CMOS RAM, it is combined with the basic BIOS stored on the ROM and then sent to RAM. This file of information is called the **boot file**. It is important to understand the difference between the boot program and the boot file. The boot program gets the system ready to accept an operating system while the boot file contains some of the parameters by which the system will operate. While the boot program is unalterable and is stored in ROM, the boot file (which the program finds and reads) is at least partly user-definable and therefore cannot be thought of as being stored on ROM.

The computer is now ready to load the OS. Generally the OS is found on the hard disk, but it will look at the A drive first to make sure there is no alternative there.

QUESTION:

Why does the computer look to the other drives before loading the perfectly usable OS from the hard disk?

Most PCs use either a command-based OS like MSDOS, which is fairly rare now, or, more commonly, a GUI-based OS like Windows. If the OS that is found is Windows, the boot program will search for IO.SYS and load it. IO.SYS holds extensions to the BIOS, including a routine called SYSINIT. This routine controls the loading of MSDOS.SYS that lies behind Windows and will work with the BIOS to manage files and execute programs.

The OS now searches for files like CONFIG.SYS, which will tell it how many files can be open at a time and which device drivers to load. After this the OS looks for a file called COMMAND.COM.

Note: Do we begin to realise why, if an exam question asks for a piece of software stored on ROM, you can't just answer 'The BIOS'?

This file contains further information about the BIOS and also some standard OS utilities.

The user can adjust the contents of the CONFIG.SYS file and a file called AUTOEXEC.BAT so that the startup is tailored to their needs.

The OS now takes control of the computer and the memory and will load jobs into the memory for processing according to the rules that we have talked about already in this section. Windows is a multi-tasking OS and will allow processing time to more than one program.

The OS must be able to find files on the storage devices and to this end it relies on the device having its own index showing where files are stored. The index on the hard drive is known as the **FAT** (file allocation table). When the surface of the disk is formatted it is divided into **sectors** and **tracks** and groups of sectors are combined into **clusters** on the disk surface.

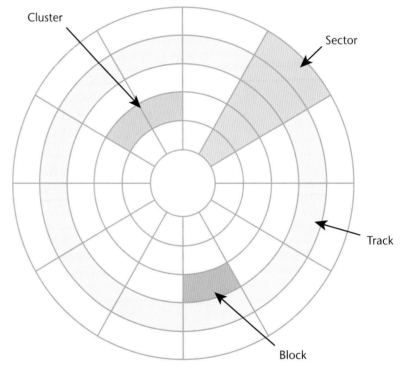

Figure 3.5

The FAT simply has all the clusters on the disk surface listed in order and the file that is stored there. Files that require multiple clusters because of their size will have the clusters linked together in the table, and clusters that are not in use will be tagged as available.

After studying Chapter 17 come back to this section and see if you can follow the diagram below, showing how files are stored as linked lists.

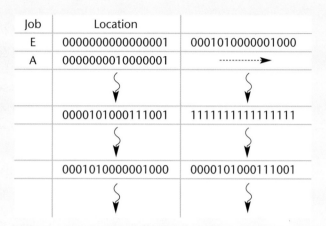

Figure 3.6

The diagram shown uses 16 bits for the pointers. What problem could this cause that might limit the storage capacity of hard drives? Why do some OSs use VFAT (known as very FAT, although it should be virtual FAT), which uses 32 bits for each entry?

Chapter 14 The Function and Purpose of Translators

1. Types of translators and their use

When computers were first invented the only way to program them was to work in binary numbers that represented the different instructions. The addresses in memory where data was being stored also had to be referred to as binary numbers. It is hardly surprising then that programming was extremely complex and could only be done by a very small number of people.

In the late 1940s a 'language' was developed which simply took each of the binary numbers that stood for instructions and allowed them to be written as groups of letters that would have some meaning to human beings. Therefore, instead of a computer needing to be given a code like 01101101 and knowing that that meant it was to add a value to the total it already had, the computer could be given ADD. This was much more convenient for human programmers and meant that more people were able to program. The computer simply had a 'lookup table' in its memory so that it could look up ADD and get 01101101. The same would be true for SUB meaning subtract from the total already calculated and MULT meaning multiply, and so on. These groups of letters are not exactly words but rather they are called **mnemonics**. There was also a problem for programmers in remembering the binary addresses where data was being stored. This could be simplified by allowing the programmers to make up names for the addresses where things were stored, such as two numbers that might be called NUM1 and NUM2, and their total being called TOT, and so on. The computer could then assign binary addresses to these pieces of data and store the addresses and the names in another lookup table. These addresses are called **labels**. An instruction and its label could be ADD NUM1, which would mean 'add whatever is in NUM1 to the value you already have'.

We now have a language that can be used to program the computer that is a lot easier to use than binary. It is a very simple language because each mnemonic and label can only mean one thing and there is a one-to-one relationship between binary operations and the mnemonics. Languages like this are called **Assembly languages** and they are low-level languages. The piece of software that can translate from one version to the other is called an **assembler** and is specific to that particular computer. The binary code created is called **machine code**.

The first languages that could go further than this were developed in the early 1950s, the first being a language called **Fortran**.

< Discuss >

Discuss how statements (referring to the syntax above) like PLINT x,y and PRINT x,y will be identified by the translator.

Explain what is meant by a **syntax error**.

Take some statements from the language that you are familiar with from your work in Unit 2. For each of the statements you have chosen, try to write down rules of syntax that the computer will follow when instructions are presented in that language. (We will return to this in Chapter 19.)

Figure 3.7

These languages differ from assembly languages in two specific ways:

- The first is that each of the instructions gives rise to a series of machine code instructions and hence is a one-to-many language. This means that the software that translates such programs must be more complex.
- Secondly, the languages can now be more portable between different machines.
- Languages like this are called **high-level languages** and programs written using them are called **source code**. When the program has been translated the result is called **object code**. The basic structure of a high-level language instruction is a special word, called the **keyword**. Each keyword is associated with a statement that has its own syntax. For example, the keyword PRINT (every language has its own keywords, so let's keep it simple) might be followed by a list of things to print out. Each item to be printed must be separated from all the others by commas. This is a very simple set of rules for an instruction and most would be far more complex. When the instruction is translated, the translator looks up the keyword in its table of keywords. (Note that if it has been spelled wrongly then the translator will fail to find it and will report an error.) When the keyword is found there will be a set of rules (the syntax for the instruction) and the translator will check the syntax against these rules before carrying on with the translation.

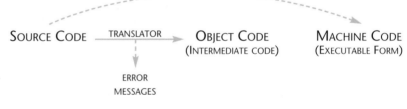

(Note: The diagram is an attempt to put in simple terms, very complex ideas. Things differ depending on the type of translator being used, and the reader is advised to regularly refer back to this diagram throughout the chapter to see how the different translators fit.)

There are three types of translator program. The first we have already seen. It is the **assembler**, which translates low-level language code into machine code. The second and third both translate high-level language code (source code) into machine code. The first of these is called the **interpreter**. This takes one line of code, translates it, lets the computer run it and then translates the next line, and so on through the rest of the code. This is very useful for finding errors in the code because when the program fails because, for instance, of a logical error, the interpreter knows precisely where the error is, because it must be at the line of code it just translated. This makes an interpreter very useful when you are developing code.

QUESTION:

Can you think of another reason for using an interpreter when developing code?

The last type takes the source code and translates it into object code before allowing it to be run. This last type is called a **compiler**. Notice that an interpreter does not create object code, but a compiler does. This means that programs that are compiled will run more quickly than programs that are interpreted because they do not have to be translated as they are being run.

QUESTION:

Can you think of another reason for using a compiler rather than an interpreter?

One problem with the translation of high-level languages is that each language has to have a different translator and every make of computer is different and requires different machine code. This means that every combination of language and computer needs a separate translator. It would be far more efficient if the compiler or interpreter only translated 'half-way' to a standard form of low-level language which could then be translated to the computer's own machine code. This 'half-way' type of language is called **intermediate code**. Intermediate code is fairly useless because it won't run without further translation to turn it into the machine code that the computer needs. But it would run on a sort of 'pretend' machine that it was designed for, although it does not exist. This is known as a **virtual machine**.

2. Lexical and syntax analysis, code generation and optimisation

These stages are the stages of compilation, when a high-level language program is translated using a compiler. Each one is done in a **parse** of the code, which is like a look-through. Each parse tells the computer something else about the program that is being translated and allows it to go on to the next level. The problem that a compiler has which is not faced by the interpreter or the assembler is that to some extent it has to understand what the code is doing in order to be able to translate it into an efficient set of instructions.

Lexical analysis

Each statement will contain a keyword that will tell the compiler what it is doing. The compiler has a table of acceptable keywords and it will look up the keyword in its table to make sure that it exists. This is where the type of error like using PLINT instead of

PRINT will be spotted because PLINT will not be in the table. As long as the keyword does exist it will replace the letters by a set of binary numbers called **tokens**, which stand for the keyword. It will then get rid of any superfluous characters like spaces that had been inserted by the programmer to make the program look prettier, or annotation which the programmer had put in to explain the logic. What is left will also be tokenised so that it ends up with a set of binary codes standing for the individual program statements. It will also spot any 'names' in the code which it does not recognise but are standing for things like variables (X, Y, TOTAL…) and it will create a lookup table, called the symbol table, so that the compiler can end up with a table of values which will tell it all about the variables that are being used. The symbol table will store the name of the variable, the data type and any restrictions on the variable. It will also store the location in the memory where the variable is stored. The contents of the table will be completed during the different parses.

Syntax analysis

During the **lexical analysis** parse, the keyword was identified and the superfluous contents of the instruction were dispensed with. During the **syntax analysis**, the compiler will use the keyword table to decide what the instruction for that particular keyword is and what the rules are for it. It will then compare what has been submitted in the code with what it should be accepting to check that it has been entered correctly. Typically, if a comma was expected after a character and a full stop had been input instead then the syntax analyser would reject it and be able to give an explanation as to why it had been rejected.

Code generation

Once the first two parses have been done, the compiler has a good idea of what is being done by each of the statements and has checked each one to ensure that it follows the rules properly. Now is the time to follow those rules and the compiler takes each statement (which is by now just a string of binary numbers) and changes them into low-level/intermediate code. This process is known as a one-to-many process because it creates many low-level instructions for each high-level one that it started with. This, in turn, means that the program will generally end up being much longer when it is in an executable form than it was in its high-level language state.

Optimisation

Optimisation is often considered a part of the code generation. Basically, after code generation there will be a set of code which, when run, will carry out the instructions in the original high-level language program. However, this set of code is almost certainly not the most efficient version that there could be and in optimisation the idea is that the compiler should get rid of any lines that are not strictly necessary so that the program is shorter, will take up less space in the memory and will run more quickly.

3. Library routines

Many short pieces of code for carrying out a particular process recur in many larger programs and it is something of a waste to go through the whole process of writing the high-level code and then compiling it every time it is used. It is therefore common practice to keep a library of routines that can be called upon whenever a particular task is necessary. These routines are pre-written, pre-compiled and pre-tested. They are loaded into the memory when a utility program called a **loader** needs them and they are linked to the relevant places in the existing code by a utility routine called a **linker**.

Chapter 15 Computer Architectures

1. Von Neumann architecture

This refers to the method of processing and design of the processor that is used in most computers. Von Neumann described a processor that took each instruction serially and performed it before carrying out the next. In addition, the instructions and data were all stored together in the same memory.

2. Registers – purpose and use, the fetch-execute cycle

In order to process the instructions in a program, a processor requires a number of special locations in which specific items need to be stored while this processing is carried out. These special locations are called **registers**. They have been described in Chapter 4.1. The registers carry out the processing by following a specific series of actions called the **fetch-execute cycle**:

- The PC holds the address of the next instruction to be carried out.
- This address is copied into the MAR.
- The contents of the address in the MAR are copied into the MDR.
- The contents of the MDR are copied into the CIR.
- The contents of the PC are incremented.

This first stage of actions is the 'fetch' part of the cycle because the instruction has been fetched and is now ready for further processing.

- The contents of the CIR are then divided into the binary code standing for the operation to be carried out, and probably the address of the data that will be used by the operation.
- The control unit then interprets the operation code so that the processor knows what to do.

This part of the cycle is sometimes called the 'decode' stage.

- The address part of the instruction is copied from CIR to MAR.
- The data found in the address in MAR is copied to MDR.
- The data is used.

This part of the cycle is called the 'execute' stage.

The final bullet point is more complex because the action depends entirely on the type of instruction. If arithmetic is to be done then the contents of the MDR are sent to the accumulator where the arithmetic is carried out. If an unconditional jump instruction is to be carried out then the contents of the MDR are copied to the PC.

< Discuss >

1 If the contents of the PC is 100 at the start of the cycle, explain how it could end up as: 101, 102, 104 and 200 at the end of the cycle.
2 Arithmetic operations are carried out by 'accumulating' values in the accumulator. How can the accumulator be used to perform the other arithmetic operations? (There are other registers that may be used, called **arithmetic registers**.)
3 How can the processor execute a conditional jump instruction, something like "Jump to address 200 if X < 0"?

< Discuss >

Discuss the meaning of the term 'array processor' and try to justify its use in a number of applications, including weather forecasting.

3. Other architectures

As we will be seeing in the next chapter, not all data or numbers are stored in the same number of bytes. Some numbers require significantly more bytes than others. A processor that is capable of processing large representations in one operation is a Maths co-processor. In Chapter 9.2 we met the concept of an array of data.

Parallel processors are a number of processors working together in order to speed up a complex processing tasks. While speeding up the processing, the disadvantage of their use is the special programming that has to be done to control the process.

These programs, however simple or special, will eventually be translated into machine code instructions, each of which will contain a specific operation code. Each type of processor, and there are many kinds, uses a specific set of operations which are specified during manufacture. One way to categorise the processors that are suitable for use in microcomputers is to indicate the number of different instructions recognised. CISC (Complex Instruction Set Computer) means a computer that can recognise and use many machine code instructions and RISC (Reduced Instruction Set Computer) uses fewer instructions. This reduction leads to generally faster processing but does mean that some instructions require a combination of simpler instructions.

< Discuss >

Discuss the effect that RISC and CISC will have on the contents of CIR.

< Activity >

Try to find out some specific types of microprocessor and determine what makes each one different from the others.

Chapter 16 Data Representation

1. Floating point binary

In Chapter 3.1, the importance of using binary to represent data, specifically numeric data, was highlighted. In that section the representation of integers, both positive and negative, was described. We now need to understand how fractions can be represented.

Consider the model of a byte that we use to store a whole number:

128	64	32	16	8	4	2	1

Effectively, there is a point at the right-hand end because you cannot have a smaller whole number than 1. Also, notice that if you start with 128 then each of the subsequent headings can be considered to be the previous one divided by two. If we were to use a two-byte representation, with the second byte coming after the point it should look like this:

So $2^3/4$ or 2.75 would be stored as:

				8	4	2	1	1/2	1/4	1/8	1/16				
0	0	0	0	0	0	1	0	1	1	0	0	0	0	0	0

Some things to notice before we go further:

1 The arrows are on the diagrams because the labelling can get extremely tedious and cumbersome.
2 The principles remain the same however many bytes we use to represent the numbers. In reality, more than 2 bytes would be used because otherwise the range of the numbers that can be represented is too small.
3 Notice that the 'point' must stay in the same place, whatever the value being represented, because the computer has no symbol with which to represent the division between integer and fractional parts of the number.

It begins to become clear that one of the major restrictions of this representation is the fact that the point cannot be moved. This type of representation will store fractions but it is clear that it has a specific problem associated with it because of the fixed position of the point.

Consider the value 2.75 or $2^3/4$ that we looked at earlier:

$$2.75 = 10.11$$

<< Discuss >>

What will happen if $2^1/3$ is to be stored in binary?

Write down some more numbers that will cause this problem.

Determine a rule that will predict whether or not the problem will occur.

This could be written as:

$10.11 = 1.011 \times 2^1$ (remember this is base 2)

or $10.11 = .1011 \times 2^{10}$

or $10.11 = .001011 \times 2^{100}$

or $10.11 = 1011. \times 2^{-10}$

(there are an infinite number of possibilities!)

Notice the point is moving. We are working towards floating point representation.

2. Normalisation of floating point binary numbers

The computer cannot cope with the point being in a different place from one number to the next because, unlike us, it has no way of representing the point. So we have to choose one of the many possibilities. It doesn't make much difference as to which possibility is chosen as long as everyone sticks to it. The representation used is the second one suggested above, the one that puts the point in front of the first 1 in the binary representation (for positive numbers).

Consider our example of $2.75 = 10.11$:

$= .1011 \times 2^{10}$

< Discuss >

Discuss the need for negative powers of 2.

Don't worry about the power of 2, as it simply states the number of places the point needs to be moved in order to give the original number.

When the value is written like this it is said to be **normalised**.

Consider the representation 0.1011×2^{10} – it consists of a number of parts.

First, there is '0.1011'. Notice the addition of the 0 in front of the point. This part of the representation contains the actual values. It is called the **mantissa** (mathematicians will know why, to the rest of us it doesn't matter!).

< Discuss >

Discuss the values that should be placed above the bits in the representation.

For each of the following use an 8-bit byte like the one above.

Discuss how $6\frac{1}{2}$ would be stored in floating point.

Discuss how $-6\frac{1}{2}$ would be stored in floating point.

Discuss how $\frac{1}{4}$ would be stored in floating point.

Next, there comes 'x' and '2'. These will always be the same, irrespective of the value being represented. As they never change there is no need to store them as part of the representation.

Finally, there is the power of 2, '10'. Remember that this could also be negative. It is called the **exponent**.

Simplifying our representation to store the value in 8 bits will give:

Mantissa					Exponent		
0	1	0	1	1	0	1	0

Consider our 8 bit representation:

−1	1/2	1/4	1/8	1/16	−4	2	1

The largest number that can be stored in this representation is 01111011, which is 0.1111×2^{11}

$$= (^1/_2 + {}^1/_4 + {}^1/_8 + {}^1/_{16}) \times 2^3$$

$$= {}^{15}/_{16} \times 8$$

$$= 7^1/_2$$

< Activity >

Work out the largest value, negative number that can be held.

What happens if we change the representation by having more bits for the exponent? The first thing is that the number available for the mantissa must go down because we still have a maximum of 8 bits we can use. Consider:

	Mantissa				Exponent		
−1	1/2	1/4	1/8	−8	4	2	1

The first thing to notice is that the most accurate any value can now be is to the nearest $^1/_8$th rather than $^1/_{16}$th; in other words the number cannot be stored so accurately.

QUESTION:

This is not quite right. The point about accuracy is correct, but what is not true?

Secondly, the largest value that can be stored is:

−1	1/2	1/4	1/8	−8	4	2	1
0	1	1	1	0	1	1	1

$$= (^1/_2 + {}^1/_4 + {}^1/_8) \times 2^{111}$$

$$= {}^7/_8 \times 2^7$$

$$= {}^7/_8 \times 128$$

$$= 112$$

This is much bigger than before.

< Discuss >

What happens when the size of the mantissa is increased?

Provide evidence for your assertions.

So, the results of increasing the number of bits for the exponent are:

1 The number of bits for the mantissa goes down.
2 The accuracy that is available is reduced.
3 The range of (size of) numbers that can be stored is increased.

Chapter 17 Data Structures and Data Manipulation

1. Implementation of data structures

A data structure is a way of storing data so that its position has meaning. 'Chris, Barbara, David, Ann' is an example of data. If the data is written as 'Ann, Barbara, Chris, David' then it has been ordered and not only does the data have meaning but so does the position of the data in the list. The data could be stored as:

Ann	David
Chris	Barbara

and this might be the structure according to the position in which they sit in a class.

In computing there are a number of structures that can be used in different circumstances. In Chapter 9 we saw the importance and the use of different file access techniques, each of which provides a loose structure to the data. The concept of an array of data was also explained. This is a rather more rigid structure than a mere file access technique; indeed, data stored in an array can be stored using many different types of access. It is difficult to see where the different types of access suddenly become data structures. A way of thinking about it is to think of file access as being logical whereas structures are more physical. That is not to say that we can touch one of these structures but we can use diagrams to visualise what they may look like. An example of this is the array that we have already studied. Memory can be thought of as looking like an enormous bookshelf with each shelf being a location in memory.

Using this simple example, it seems silly to scatter the data about because all the data has something in common – they are people in a class. So why don't we put all that data together in the same place?

A problem that arises is that the amount of memory which will be needed for the array must be specified before you start so that the required locations can be reserved, otherwise when you want to put the data in there may not be enough contiguous locations left. How much should we reserve? In this case if Ewan comes into the class there is no space left in the array, so perhaps we should start with 5 locations being reserved. However big we make it, it is always possible that this is a very popular class and we may need another space! If we go for 100 locations then there shouldn't be a need for any more (but there may be!) However, in this particular case, with only 4 in the class, 96 locations are wasted

< Discuss >

Discuss the importance in this example of knowing where the front of the room is.

Address	
1	
2	
3	
4	
5	
6	
7	ANN
8	
9	
10	
11	
12	
13	
14	DAVID
15	
16	
17	
18	
19	
20	
21	CHRIS
22	
23	
24	
25	BARBARA
26	

Note: Data is held in locations 7, 14, 21, 25

Figure 3.8 Diagram of memory showing how data is scattered around

< Discuss >

Discuss the addresses in the diagram.

ARRAYCLASS()

Address	
1	
2	
3	
4	
5	
6	
7	
8	
9	
10	ANN
11	DAVID
12	CHRIS
13	BARBARA
14	
15	
16	
17	
18	
19	
20	

Note: ARRAYCLASS() is a one-dimensional array of size 4, containing text data and is located at address 10.

The data is stored in CLASS(0), CLASS(1), CLASS(2), CLASS(3).

These now become data addresses.

Figure 3.9 Diagram of an array

because they have been reserved and can't be used for anything else. Like so many things in Computing, a decision has to be made and a compromise decided upon.

Notice that the decisions about the array – data type, size and shape (number of dimensions) and name – must be made before it is used. Once these decisions are made they cannot be changed, and consequently this is a static data structure.

Some of the problems with static structures can be solved by finding a way to allow them to be changed during use (note the difference between 'changing the data' and 'changing the structure').

A simple one-dimensional array is called a **list** and if we draw the contents of the array slightly differently we can see the important parts of an array.

A list can be represented by the following diagrams:

Address		HEAD_OF_LIST= 7.
1		
2		
3		
4		
5		
6		
7	ANN 14	
8		
9		
10		
11		
12		
13		
14	DAVID 21	
15		
16		
17		
18		
19		
20		
21	CHRIS 25	
22		
23		
24		
25	BARBARA X	
26		

Figure 3.10 List with data held serially

Address		HEAD_OF_LIST= 7.
1		
2		
3		
4		
5		
6		
7	ANN 25	
8		
9		
10		
11		
12		
13		
14	DAVID X	
15		
16		
17		
18		
19		
20		
21	CHRIS 14	
22		
23		
24		
25	BARBARA 21	
26		

Figure 3.11 List with data held sequentially by alphabetical order

< Discuss >

Discuss the probable make-up of the 'HEAD_OF_LIST'. Originally, the array was called CLASS, but where is this now? Is it important?

In each version of the list discuss the stages necessary to find CHRIS.

< Discuss >

Using the lists CLASS and FREE, discuss how CHARLES can be added to the CLASS list. Discuss how CHRIS can be removed from the list when he leaves the class.

Does it make any difference if the list is held serially or sequentially? What problems arise if EWAN or ALANNA need to be added to the CLASS?

What happens if all the students leave the class?

The numbers after the data are called **pointers** and this is because they point to the next data item.

Some of the available spaces for data in memory will be used up by lists like this one, some will be used up by other data structures and some will not yet be in use. The locations that are not yet being used are linked together in their own list called the FREE_SPACE_LIST. So, our fragment of memory may now look like this:

Address			
ARRAY ROOMS()	1		
	2		
	3		
	4		
	5		
	6		
	7	ANN	25
	8		9
	9		10
	10		11
	11		20
	12		13
	13		X
	14	DAVID	X
	15		
ARRAY ACHERS()	16		
	17		
	18		
	19		
	20		26
	21	CHRIS	14
	22		23
	23		24
	24		12
	25	BARBARA	21
	26		22

HEAD_OF_LIST
CLASS= 7
FREE_SPACE_LIST= 8

Figure 3.12 Design of memory fragment with other structures and free space

< Discuss >

What advantages are lost when restricting a dynamic structure within a static structure?

This sort of data structure is called a **linked list** for fairly obvious reasons. The size of a linked list, unlike an array, does not have to be stated before the start of processing and hence it is called a **dynamic data structure**. Our examples here have all been created in a small area of memory which may well be an array itself, so be aware that a dynamic structure like this one can be stored within a static structure.

Address				
8				
9				
10	DAVID	X	CLASS(0)	
11		(3)	CLASS(1)	
12	ANN	(7)	CLASS(2)	
13		(5)	CLASS(3)	
14	CHRIS	(0)	CLASS(4)	
15		(6)	CLASS(5)	
16		(8)	CLASS(6)	
17	BARBARA	(4)	CLASS(7)	
18		(9)	CLASS(8)	
19		X	CLASS(9)	
20				
21				

ARRAYCLASS(0)=10
HEAD_OF_LIST
CLASS=CLASS(2)
FREE=CLASS(1)

Figure 3.13 A linked list being stored within the static data structure of an array

When a list or an array can only be added to at one end and have values removed from the other then it becomes an essentially serial structure as the position is related to the chronological appearance of the data rather than any quality of the data itself.

This type of structure is called a **queue**.

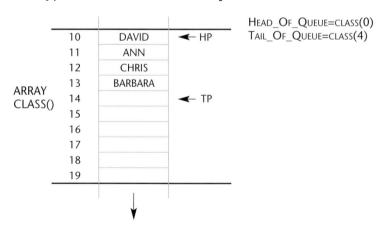

HEAD_OF_QUEUE=CLASS(0)
TAIL_OF_QUEUE=CLASS(4)

Figure 3.14 A queue being stored in an array

< Discuss >

Some questions to discuss:

1 Try to explain what is happening when data is read from a queue. Why is it still there? (Is it still there?)

2 **a)** Try to create an algorithm (2 lines can be enough) to describe the process of adding data to a queue.

b) If this process continues, the tail pointer will 'hit' the end of the array. What can happen?

3 Try to define tests to determine whether a queue is:

a) full

b) empty.

What major problem can arise if either case arises?

Figure 3.15

Note that because the next value to be used is the one that has been there the longest and the next to be placed on the queue needs to go on the other end, we need two pointers. In this text, the pointers are known as the head and tail pointers and they point to the next value to be used and the next space that can be used. In other texts the way the pointers are arranged can be different – they may have slightly different names, or point at the last value in the queue rather than at the first free space. It doesn't matter – just be consistent. Imagine that the data DAVID has been read and EWAN has been added; the result is shown in Figure 3.15.

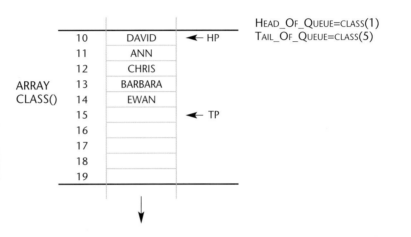

A stack is a bit like a queue but data is read from the same end as it arrives. The following diagrams illustrate this:

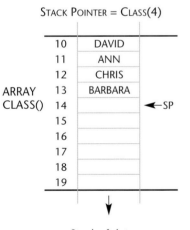

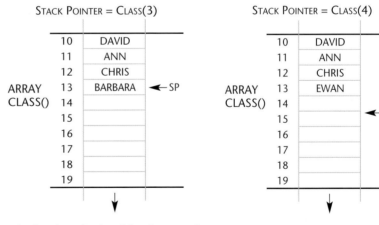

Stack of data *Stack after data (Barbara) has been read* *Stack after data (Ewan) has been added*

Figure 3.16

Chapter 17 Data Structures and Data Manipulation

159

< Discuss >

How could the data 'DAVID' be read from the stack while still keeping all the other data items in the stack?

Try to develop simple algorithms, which will reverse the order of the values being held in a queue or a stack using only stack and queue, and read and write.

< Activity >

Describe how values are:

a) added to

b) removed from

a stack.

Notice the way that when either structure is read, it is a copy that is read, and the data is not removed from the array until it is overwritten.

A **tree** is a structure in which data can be held. Each item of data points to two others and a rule is needed for determining the route taken from any data item. The data items are held in **nodes** and the possible routes are **paths**. Each node has two possible paths and the nodes are arranged in **layers**. Finally, the first node is called the **root**. Imagine the people in the class: David, Barbara, Chris, Ann, Ewan. We start on layer 1 with David as the root:

DAVID

Items of data are inserted in trees at nodes and this first one is called the **root node**. For all subsequent layers we need a rule. As this is a text list, alphabetical sounds sensible. So, if the next name is higher in the alphabet go right; if it is lower go left. The next name is Barbara, so go left:

DAVID
/
BARBARA

The next name is Chris. This is lower in the alphabet than David so we need to go left to Barbara. Chris is higher than Barbara, so go right:

DAVID
/
BARBARA
\
CHRIS

If we now add Ann (left of David, left of Barbara) and Ewan (right of David) we get:

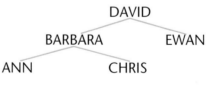

It is possible to have trees that have more than two routes out of a node but they are not as useful in computer science. Trees that are limited to a maximum of two routes out of a node are called **Binary Trees**.

< Activity >

1 Draw binary trees, using the following data to populate them, and using alphabetical order as a rule:
   a) NILE, THAMES, GANGES, AMAZON, ORINOCO, YANGTZE
   b) BREAD, COFFEE, MILK, SUGAR, TEA

2 Explain how CONGO could be inserted in the tree in 1a.

3 Devise a simple rule and store the following ID codes in trees:
   a) 1012, 2379, 1963, 1006, 2129
   b) E273, D618, D391, G602, E196, E398

< Discuss >

Discuss the results to Question 1.

We have to ask the question: 'Why bother?'

There are a number of ways of reading a tree, one of which we will look at here. We need rules and this particular set of rules is as follows:

At each node:

1 If there is a left branch that has not been traversed (followed) yet, then follow it and repeat.
2 Read the node if not already read.
3 If there is a right branch, traverse it and repeat.
4 Go back up one layer.

Application of these rules to our original tree gives:

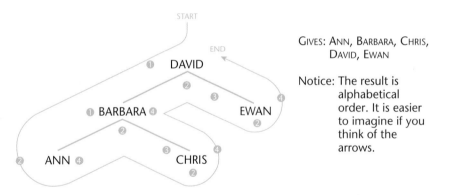

GIVES: ANN, BARBARA, CHRIS, DAVID, EWAN

Notice: The result is alphabetical order. It is easier to imagine if you think of the arrows.

Figure 3.17

Use this algorithm to read the other trees you have created.

Trees can be stored in arrays by using two pointers for each data item. The first pointer points to the left node in the next layer, while the second points to the right node in the next layer. If there is no link then the null value is inserted.

< Activity >

Try to develop an algorithm for reading the array versions of the trees.

The example of class names would give:

DAVID	1	4	0
BARBARA	3	2	1
CHRIS	X	X	2
ANN	X	X	3
EWAN	X	X	4
			5
			6
			7
			8
			9

CLASS()   ROOT NODE = 0

Deleting data from a tree is more difficult than it would at first seem. Consider removing Barbara from our tree. How can we now find anyone who is 'below' Barbara's layer? Not only was BARBARA an item of data, but it was also an integral part of the tree structure.

< Discuss >

Discuss how to insert FIONA and ALAN into this representation of the tree. Create array representations for the other trees.

< Discuss >

How could BARBARA be deleted while maintaining the integrity of the tree? (There are two accepted ways of doing this.)

2. Searching, merging and sorting

(Serial and Binary searching were covered in Chapter 9.)

If two files are being used and it becomes necessary to combine them, it is a straightforward process if the files are simple serial files, because order does not matter and so one file can simply be appended to the end of the other.

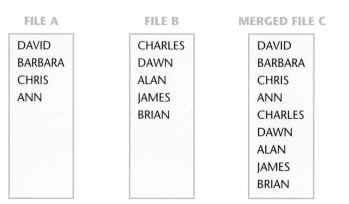

FILE A	FILE B	MERGED FILE C
DAVID	CHARLES	DAVID
BARBARA	DAWN	BARBARA
CHRIS	ALAN	CHRIS
ANN	JAMES	ANN
	BRIAN	CHARLES
		DAWN
		ALAN
		JAMES
		BRIAN

Figure 3.18

However, if order is to be preserved then a more complex algorithm is needed:

```
READ FIRST VALUE FROM EACH FILE
REPEAT
  COMPARE
  WRITE SMALLEST VALUE TO NEW FILE
  READ NEXT VALUE FROM FILE USED
UNTIL NO MORE VALUES IN THAT FILE
WRITE REMAINDER OF OTHER FILE TO NEW FILE
```

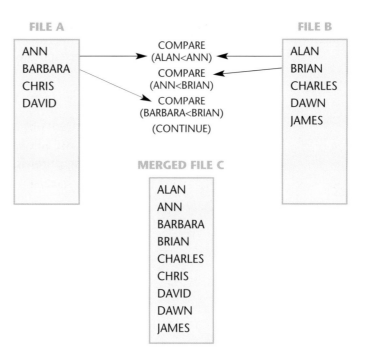

Figure 3.19

Notice that there is a specific difference in the requirements of the original files in the two examples of the merge routine. In the first example the original files are not in order, while in the second example the values in the files are in alphabetical order.

In Chapter 9 we saw the difference made to searching algorithms by the use of ordered rather than unordered files. It is not always useful to sort a file, however, if it is, then there are many ways to produce a specific order. The different methods vary in value depending on the use to which the file may be put, the number of items in the file, how well sorted the file already is, the hardware available and many other factors. The specification that we are studying specifies two types of sort technique.

a) Insertion sort

Imagine copying the contents of the file to another location. Each item in the file that is copied across is simply copied into the correct location.

The result is a file that has its contents in the correct order. This is terribly time consuming and you would not want to do it very often.

b) Quick sort

This one seems extremely cumbersome, slow and complicated, but for large files it is actually very efficient and the algorithm for carrying it out is also easy to program.

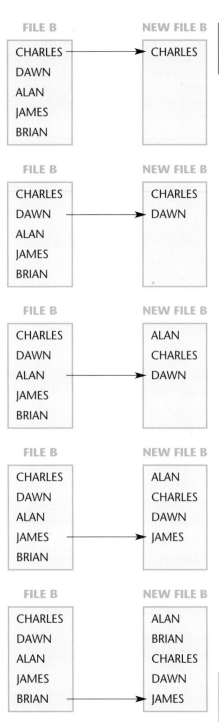

FILE B → **NEW FILE B**

FILE B	NEW FILE B
CHARLES →	CHARLES
DAWN	
ALAN	
JAMES	
BRIAN	

FILE B	NEW FILE B
CHARLES	CHARLES
DAWN →	DAWN
ALAN	
JAMES	
BRIAN	

FILE B	NEW FILE B
CHARLES	ALAN
DAWN	CHARLES
ALAN →	DAWN
JAMES	
BRIAN	

FILE B	NEW FILE B
CHARLES	ALAN
DAWN	CHARLES
ALAN	DAWN
JAMES →	JAMES
BRIAN	

FILE B	NEW FILE B
CHARLES	ALAN
DAWN	BRIAN
ALAN	CHARLES
JAMES	DAWN
BRIAN →	JAMES

Figure 3.20 An insertion sort

< Activity >

When you understand the algorithm, try to program it.

There are a set of stages to be followed:

1   Place the contents to be sorted in a row with an arrow under the first and last values, pointing at each other. (One is a 'fixed' arrow and the other is 'movable'.)

CHARLES	DAWN	ALAN	JAMES	BRIAN
⇒				←

2   IF the two values are in the correct order THEN move the 'movable' arrow towards the 'fixed' arrow. ELSE swap the items and arrows.

BRIAN	DAWN	ALAN	JAMES	CHARLES
→				⇐

3   REPEAT stage 2 UNTIL the two arrows coincide:

BRIAN	DAWN	ALAN	JAMES	CHARLES
	→			⇐

BRIAN	CHARLES	ALAN	JAMES	DAWN
	⇒			←

BRIAN	CHARLES	ALAN	JAMES	DAWN
	⇒		←	

BRIAN	CHARLES	ALAN	JAMES	DAWN
	⇒	←		

BRIAN	ALAN	CHARLES	JAMES	DAWN
	→	⇐		

BRIAN	ALAN	CHARLES	JAMES	DAWN
		⇐ →		

We now have one value (CHARLES) in the correct place, and the effect has been to split the original file into two smaller ones. The whole process is now repeated for each of the two files on either side of CHARLES. This is repeated until all the 'files' are of length 1. At this point, the file has been sorted.

< Activity >

Find out about an alternative quick sort method which uses 'pivots' and complete an algorithm to carry it out.

Have a look at some other sort techniques.

Chapter 18 High-level Language Programming Paradigms

1. Declarative programming

In Chapter 14 language methods and techniques were described in some detail. The instructions were comprehensive, sequential and specified what to do to solve a problem. This is a particular type of language called a **procedural** language – there are other types.

The first languages to be developed were low-level languages. They have a direct relationship with the machine code of the computers for which they are designed. We will be looking at these in more detail in Chapter 20.

Another programming paradigm (method of programming) is called a **declarative** programming language. In a declarative program, the computer is given a set of facts:

2G (John)	2F (Deidre)	2F (Hal)
2F (Jane)	2G (Val)	2G (Don)

and a goal, for instance:

2G(X) means 'find all instances of a member of 2G'.

If it is run then the computer applies the definitions to the facts and supplies the results: John, Val, Don.

A declarative language does not need a set of instructions but is capable of deciding how to solve the problem presented.

< Activity >

Using the idea of a school and types of information that would be stored in a school, like the example above, come up with a set of facts and different rules for eliciting different results. For each rule, state the results and explain how they would be arrived at.

If the rules are more complicated then the searching can become more complex.

Imagine more facts being available:

male (John)	male (Hal)	male (Don)
female (Deidre)	female (Val)	female (Jane)

and additional definitions:

male (x) means that x is male

female (x) means that x is female

If we want to find members of 2F who are male, this is called a **goal**. We want male (x), 2F (x).

The computer will search its facts for a male. It finds John.

This value is an **instance** of male. It can now look in the other set of facts and finds that John is not in 2F.

This is a failure and it has to return to the original set of facts. This is called **backtracking** – one possibility has failed, so start again.

This time, Hal is found to be male and when the second set of facts is checked, 2F is found to be true. The goal, to find a male in 2F has been satisfied.

All the other facts would be checked to ensure there were no other instances of success.

< Activity >

Explain the stages in finding:

2F (x), male (x)
female (x), 2G (x)

Predicate logic is the name for this type of process, when different facts are applied to rules and the result can be considered true or false.

2. Object-oriented programming

Another programming paradigm is **object-oriented** programming, sometimes called OOP.

OOP relies on objects in the real world being classified. Like most people I live in a dwelling. There is a basic similarity with all dwellings – they all have addresses for instance. Sometimes it is necessary to use that address, and to do so we need a method to access it. These facts can be illustrated on a generalised diagram to show dwellings:

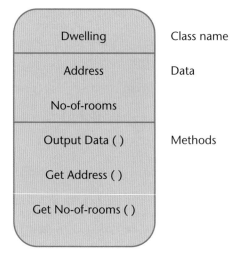

Dwelling	Class name
Address	Data
No-of-rooms	
Output Data ( )	Methods
Get Address ( )	
Get No-of-rooms ( )	

Figure 3.21

This shows the information about a group of things that have the same characteristics. The group is called a **class**. My house is an object that is a member of that class. Your dwelling is also an object of the class 'Dwelling'.

The objects can only provide data, like address, from within the class. This concept of only accessing data through the methods of the class is known as **data encapsulation**.

My dwelling is a house. There are other types of dwelling: bungalow, flat, etc. House, bungalow and flat are types of dwelling, but they are very different from each other and may have specific properties. Each should be its own class:

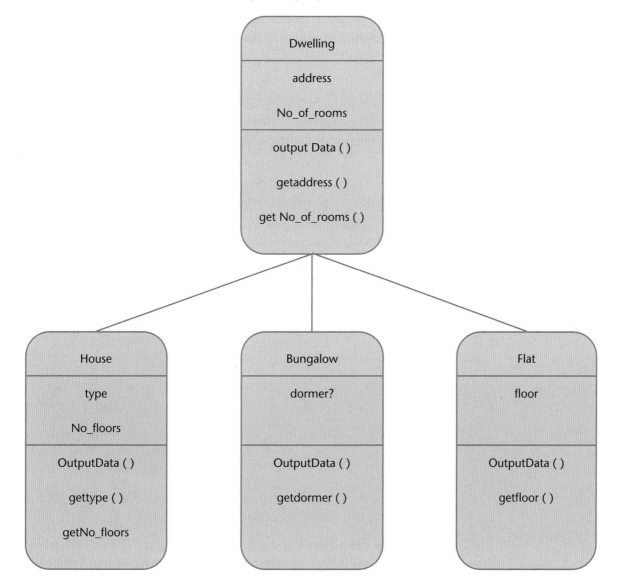

Figure 3.22

Each of these three classes is different, shown by the different types of data that are stored, but each one has its address and number of rooms held in the Dwelling class because they are relevant to all classes. There is a hierarchy here. 'Dwelling' is a superclass because others can use its data and those that use it, such as House, Bungalow and Flat are subclasses or **derived classes**. The derived classes have **inherited** this data from the superclass.

Object-oriented languages are complex languages and methods have had to be developed which can be used to define and explain the solutions that are produced. This methodology for planning and explaining object-oriented programming is called the **Unified Modelling Language** (UML).

UML consists of a number of descriptive diagrammatic representations that describe the stages required to produce object-oriented programs.

Do not worry about this section. The diagrams tend to be simple to understand and questions will tend to be expecting an understanding of and an interpretation of diagrams given on the paper.

We have already seen an example of a class diagram in Figure 3.22. All classes must have objects that are members of the class, otherwise what is the point of defining the class?

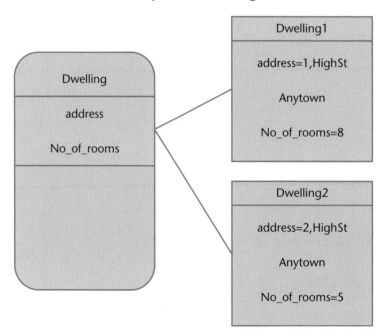

Figure 3.23

This sort of diagram shows the attributes for specific objects from a class. It is called an **object diagram**.

A **use case** diagram shows what is happening in a system rather than how it is done. Users are depicted outside the box and processes over which they have some control are shown and linked within the box.

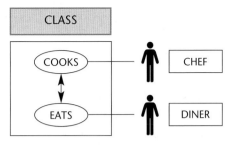

Figure 3.24

A **state diagram** shows the state of an object through the process, while **activity diagrams** are like a flowchart showing how the logic behind the work has developed.

Chapter 19 Programming Techniques

1. Standard programming techniques

Most problems are so complex that it is not possible to solve them as a single entity. Because of this it is common to split a problem up and to solve each of the parts separately. These separate parts are called **procedures** and **functions** and we met them back in Unit 2.

Apart from making the solutions to problems easier because it is simpler to solve a lot of small problems rather than one big problem, it also allows a number of programmers to be involved in the solution at the same time, each of whom can be given a task which is particularly apposite to their abilities.

Consider the computerised production of a student's school report. It is the type of problem that would be very difficult to solve, or even think about in its entirety, but it can be split into a series of tasks that makes it very much easier because it becomes the result of solving a series of steps.

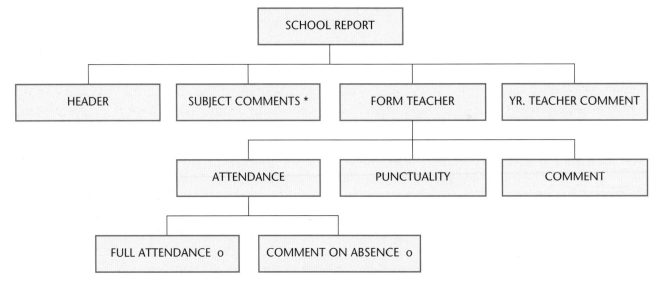

Figure 3.25

This is yet another type of diagram to add to the long list we saw in Chapter 18. The 'order' is to read from top to bottom and left to right. Some of the boxes are interchangeable, but some are not (you could not put subject comments on before the header has been done or it would not be possible to know who the comment referred to.) The * means that that box must be repeated a number of times and the o means that only one will be done.

< Discuss >

Discuss the logic of the diagram and ensure that you understand it.

Consider a building firm with a number of employees. Each employee works a variable number of hours a week. Anything over 40 hours or any Saturday or Sunday work is paid at a different rate. Tax at a flat rate of 22% must be deducted from payments. Results of an employee's weekly wage must be output to a payslip, a cheque or an email to a bank account, and a record in the employee's file. Discuss and draw a diagram like the one on the previous page for this scenario.

< Discuss >

Why is this type of approach sometimes called a top-down approach and why is the problem solution said to exhibit stepwise refinement?

< Activity >

For each of the two scenarios described in this section, identify sensible:

■ local variables
■ global variables
■ parameters passed by value
■ parameters passed by reference.

Figure 3.26

This type of approach is sometimes called a **top-down approach** and the problem solution is said to exhibit **stepwise refinement**.

If the solution is being programmed then each of the boxes is going to make up an individual procedure or function in the main program.

< Activity >

Find out the distinction between a procedure and a function. Discuss why the solution may not work despite all the individual modules, represented by the boxes, working perfectly.

In a computer solution each of the procedures need to have some data to work with. These data are called the **parameters** if they are called at the same time as the procedure. There are two ways of telling the system what these values are. One is to give the data as part of the statement, for example RECTANGLE (3,4). This is called passing the parameters by value. The alternative is to give the locations where the values can be found, for example RECTANGLE (x,y). If the values x and y are defined as local variables then the parameters are still being passed by value because any changes made to them will not be allowed to affect their values outside the procedure. When the procedure is exited the original values of x and y will be reinstated. However, if the values of x and y are global variables then any changes made during the execution of the procedure will be carried back to the calling program when the procedure is exited and the parameters are said to have been passed by reference.

The procedure may also be programmed with variables. There are two types of variable that can be used. One exists only within that particular procedure and is called a **local variable** and the other exists throughout the whole solution and is called a **global variable**. The clashing of local variables is the main cause of a problem that we mentioned earlier, that is, when modules are combined, they cause programs to crash.

There is a problem when a procedure is called and there is already a program being run. This is not really a problem as long as the computer remembers how to get back to where it came from after the procedure is finished.

Imagine a program running:

This is simple if there is only one return address to remember, but what about if the situation looks like this:

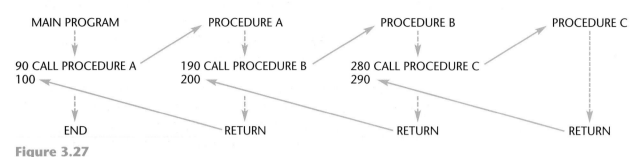

Figure 3.27

< Discuss >

Discuss whether a stack or a queue data structure should be used to store the return addresses. Justify your choice of structure.

A problem can arise if there are too many calls before it begins to unwrap. Describe the problem and discuss how the problem can be solved.

There is a problem with sending other values like parameters and the results of functions back and forth. Discuss how this could be done.

This time there are three numbers to store – the addresses 100, 200 and 290, so that the return jumps can be made. This is no problem because these return addresses can be stored in a data structure.

2. Methods for defining syntax

English is a spoken language and, like all other spoken languages, it has evolved and continues to evolve. If we went back four hundred years we would find it difficult to understand the people, or to make ourselves understood. Just have a look at the language used in a Shakespearean play. We tend to think that it is difficult to follow but at the time it was the language everyone used. Computer languages are not like that. They do not evolve, but are invented. The closest to this in a human language is Latin as it has a rigid structure and virtually unbreakable rules of syntax. As invented languages, the people who invented them had to follow rules and stick to them, otherwise other people would become confused, but, worse, the translator programs would not be able to translate them.

These rules are language-specific. In Visual Basic a FOR loop to loop from 1 to 5 would be:

FOR count = 1 to 5

in C++ the same instruction would be:

for (count = 1, count <= 5, count ++)

The two statements do the same thing but the rules that the two languages follow are very different and the translator for one would reject the other.

Almost everything that is used in a computer language has to be defined; we will look at two methods of producing those definitions. The first is BNF, which stands for **Backus-Naur Form**. Try to find out more about who invented it. The second is a method called **syntax diagrams**.

In either method, it is important to have some fixed 'definites' that are not subject to rules; these are called **terminal symbols**.

Terminal symbols are things like the letters A, B, etc. The word CAT is a combination of letters, so it could be defined as: letter, letter, letter, but a C cannot be defined as a combination of anything, as it is already as small as you can get. Other terminal symbols that we need are the digits 0, 1, 2, etc. and the mathematical symbols +, -, *, /. There are others but these will do for now.

The importance of these two methods is to take these terminal symbols and combine them in order to produce other things. Let us take, as an example, a word. In order to define a word we must first define what letters it can be made from, that is, we must define what a letter is. In BNF anything that is defined is put in angle brackets, so we want to define <LETTER>.

Imagine letter is defined by:

<LETTER>::=A | B | C | D

(Explanation: The symbol ::= means 'is defined as' and | means 'or'.)

Once something has been defined it can be used to define something else.

<WORD> ::= <LETTER> <LETTER>

This would mean that AB was defined as a word but that A or ABC was not, because we have specified that a word must have two letters. We could define word as:

<WORD> ::=<LETTER>|<LETTER><LETTER>|<LETTER> <LETTER><LETTER>

This means that A, AB, ABC are all defined as words, but what about ABCD, or others like BACADBA?

< Activity >

Work out why <WORD>::= <LETTER>|<LETTER> <WORD> will include all these possibilities.

Try to define a sentence, given that <STOP> : : = .

Explain why abc, CAT, 2BC are not words.

Using the variables:

<DIGIT> ::= 0,1,2,3,4,5,6,7,8,9

<SIGN> ::= + ?-

define a <SIGNED INTEGER>.

(Hints: Define INTEGER first. Be careful of the zero.)

Note that our final definition of word is recursive, because <WORD> is defined in terms of itself. Try to prove that CAB is a word by showing the stages in arriving at its definition.

The other method is to use a syntax diagram. The same rules about starting with terminal symbols apply here, but, after that, the structure is shown as a diagram. The rules are to always start on the left and end at the right by following the arrows.

So, following our example for BNF, we will define a letter first.

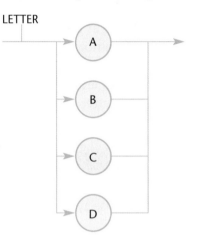

Figure 3.28

Notice that undefined, terminal symbols are normally put into circles.

Figure 3.29

This will allow us to loop as often as we like, by following the looping arrow, so a word can have as many letters as we want.

< Activity >

Draw a syntax diagram for a sentence.

Draw syntax diagrams to define:
DIGIT, INTEGER and SIGNED INTEGER.

One part of the work that a computer needs to carry out is the evaluation of algebraic expressions like X = A + B. Unfortunately, computers are unable to follow our logic (which is called **infix notation** because the sign (+) goes between the two things to be added). We would say 'A plus B'. We could equally well say 'add A and B' (this would give +AB and is called **prefix notation** because the sign goes before the things to be added). Alternatively we could say 'take A and B and add them' (this would give AB+ and is called **postfix notation**). This last, postfix, notation is also called **reverse Polish notation**.

< Activity >

Find out why postfix notation is called reverse Polish notation.

A + B becomes A B + in reverse Polish.

< Activity >

Change A-B, A*B, A/B into reverse Polish.

2 * (A + B) becomes 2 * (AB+)   (do the bracket first)

   that becomes 2 (AB+) *   (then remove the bracket)

   2AB+*

An important feature of reverse Polish is that no brackets are needed because there is never any ambiguity about the order in which things should be done.

< Activity >

Explain why 2* (A + B ^ 2) = 2 A B 2 ^ + * in reverse Polish.

Turn these expressions into reverse Polish:

(i) (A + B) * 2

(ii) (A + B) * (C + D)

(iii) 2 * A + (B + C)/2

(iv) A + A + A + A

A computer evaluates algebraic expressions using a stack. The rule is that variables and constants are put on the stack while an operator is done to the two top things in the stack with the result being put back in the stack.

Consider 2 A B + *

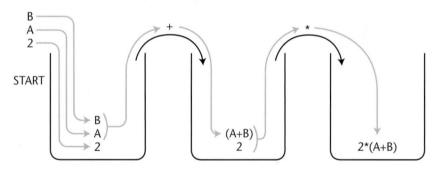

Figure 3.30

The answer is the last thing in the stack.

< Activity >

By drawing diagrams like the one above, show that the answers that you got for the Activity on the previous page are correct because they unravel to give the original infix expressions.

A major use of binary trees (Chapter 17) is to produce reverse Polish from infix expressions.

Chapter 20 Low-level Languages

1. Use of computer architecture

In Chapter 4 we learned about the different busses and how they are used, along with the special registers (PC, MR, MDR, CIR, Accumulator) to carry out instructions in the processor.

Chapter 15.2 brought the use of the registers together in a description of the fetch-execute cycle. We will return to this in order to understand the effects of the cycle on different types of instruction. We shall also look at the ways that the cycle changes according to the requirements of the instruction.

First, we need to look at the way data is stored in memory.

Imagine that memory is like a set of shelves. Each shelf is labelled (from 1 to 10) so that we can keep a record of where things are stored.

Figure 3.31

Imagine that the first instruction is stored in location 5. This location would be stored in the PC and when the program was run, that instruction would be fetched and the value in the PC would be incremented so that it pointed to the next instruction. This will take up a lot of space in the memory but we will also need a lot of other data to be held. The memory is obviously going to need to be a lot larger than this.

We will return to look again at memory use after the next section.

2. Features of low-level languages

Computers work with machine code instructions that are written as a series of binary digits. Each instruction can be thought of as being in two parts; an operation code and an address.

The computer is capable of carrying out a number of different operations and each computer can have a different operation set, so when we are discussing low-level languages we are certainly talking about machine-oriented languages. Each operation is represented by a binary code.

Imagine a machine that uses 8 bits for an instruction. This is unreasonably small but allows us to understand the process more easily. If 3 bits are used to stand for the operation code then only 8 different operations are possible.

Imagine that ADD is represented as 001. SUB stands for subtract and 010.

There are more, but that is enough for the moment.

We used 3 bits to stand for the operation, so we have 5 bits left to stand for whatever we want to ADD or SUB. This will normally be the identifier of the location in the memory where the data is being stored. This is called the **address**.

So 00101001 means ADD whatever is in address 01001 or ADD what is in address 9 (to the value in the accumulator already).

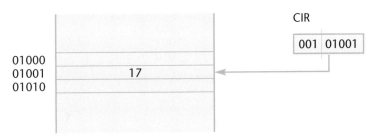

Figure 3.32

In this case, 17 will be added to the accumulator.

This is known as **direct addressing** because the address in the instruction is the address of the data to be used.

The largest address for data that can be used is 11111 in our example. This is 31, so we can only access a tiny amount of the memory. One way to solve this problem so that we can access more of the memory is to use more bits to store the address. It may be sensible to use 32 bits for each instruction. If we use 12 bits for the operation code so there are plenty of things which the computer can recognise, then we reserve 4 bits for other uses which we will see later. That leaves 16 bits for the memory address. That will allow us to address 65536 locations in the memory, which is a bit more realistic. However, we will eventually run out of addresses despite making the length of the instruction longer, so direct addressing needs supplementing with other methods.

The first alternative is to put the value to be used in the instruction:

Figure 3.33

In this case 01001 (or 9) will be added to the accumulator.

This is called **immediate addressing**; it means that the value in the instruction is not an address at all. This may look simple but the program parameters cannot be altered. With this method you can't write a program to add two numbers together, only to add 7 and 9!

Another alternative is to store the real address in the memory so that the value in the address part of the instruction is pointing to the address of the data. This is called **indirect addressing** and is a simple idea if looked at on a diagram. (With all these methods of addressing, you are encouraged to draw diagrams to illustrate answers in exam papers.)

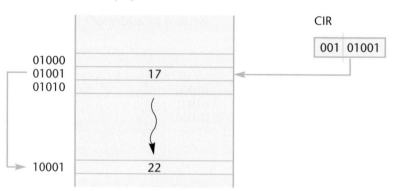

Figure 3.34

This time 22 will be added to the accumulator. This addressing method is useful because the amount of space in a location in memory is much bigger than the space in the address part of the instruction. This means that we can store much bigger addresses and hence use more memory.

The next method is called **relative addressing**. In this method direct addressing is used, but it does not commence from the start of the addresses of the memory; the addressing begins from some arbitrary fixed point. For example, imagine that the starting point is 100000.

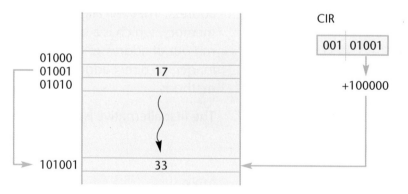

Figure 3.35

In this case 33 would be added to the accumulator.

QUESTION:

In Chapter 13 we discussed paging and segmentation. How can relative addressing be used with these methods of memory management?

The final method in our specification is called **indexed addressing**. In this method the address part of the instruction is added to a value held in a special register that we have not yet met, called the IR (**Index register**). The result is the required address.

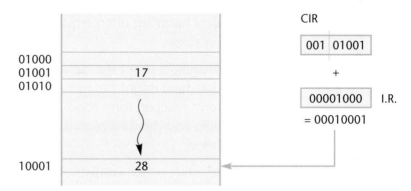

Figure 3.36

In this case the value 28 would be added to the accumulator.

Throughout this section 001 and ADD have been used interchangeably. 001 is computer-understandable but, faced with a mass of bits, a human being finds it difficult to understand. For that reason labels are attached to the binary codes; ADD is an example. These labels are called **mnemonics**. The addresses are also given codes like NUM1 and NUM2 so that we can keep track of what variable is where!

A low-level language instruction may well appear, such as ADDNUM2. The first thing the computer does is translate it into binary using a translator program called an **assembler**, so ADDNUM2 may well become 00101001.

< Discuss >

Why is indexed addressing important? What value should be placed in the IR? When using indexed addressing, how is the address part of the instruction handled?

Earlier in the chapter it was decided that some bits would be needed for another task. Try to decide what they could be used for.

Try to invent other models of addressing.

Chapter 21 Databases

1. Database design and normalisation

A **file** is a collection of sets of similar data called **records**. Each item of data within a record is called an **item** and the areas where the items are stored are called **fields** (Chapters 2.1 and 9.2).

A **database** consists of a series of related files and when these files are part of a database they are called **tables**.

Many problems are solved using simple files while more complex data handling often requires the additional structure offered by a database.

Imagine a file of the details of students in a school. Some of the data held might be: name, address, emergency contact, form, form teacher, form room, subjects studied, etc. Each of these is a field and the data placed in them is the item. So in this case we have:

- a file, which consists of all the data about all the pupils in the school
- records, each of which has the same sort of contents and each one relates to a specific student
- records that are divided up into areas for the individual pieces of information, so each student will have a record that contains their name, their address, and so on
- fields, which may have an item of data in them or not. The name field is always going to be full, but if a field existed to contain 'team played for' then this may be blank as presumably some students do not play for any team.

Some of the fields here may be unique, for instance it is possible (though unlikely) that all the students have different names, but this certainly cannot be guaranteed. Some fields will not cause a problem when the data is stored, and some may be very useful, for instance the address field may be used as part of a mail merge for contacting a particular, geographic group, such as all those who live in a particular village. Some will be repeated in record after record, for example all students in the same form will have the same form teacher and form room. The subjects studied by students will be of an indeterminate length and will cause the same sort of problem as the 'team played for' field discussed above.

Each record in a file must be identifiable and consequently there must be at least one field in each record that can be guaranteed to be unique. In this way it can be used to identify the record. Typically, something like an account number or a membership number is used. In the school example it will be a school number,

< Discuss >

The advantages and disadvantages of using a database to store data rather than using flat files.

< Discuss >

Why may the suggested field 'team played for' cause a problem? How would you solve this problem?

< Discuss >

How can these problems be overcome? Discuss the need for both fixed length and variable length records.

and it may also be an examination number, which is unique across the whole country, let alone in the school. Whichever field it is, it is special and is known as the **primary**, or **key field**.

Consider your list of fields and decide which will have the same data in a number of records. These will have to be moved to be in other files. An example would be form teacher and form room, which could be in another file linked to this one by form. If we wanted to know about a student's form we just use the link to go to the form file and then search for the record that has that form as its primary key. This is a key field in one file (the form file) that is being used as a link to another file (the student file). This key field is called a **foreign key** when it is in a file where it is not the key but is providing a link.

We should now be comfortable with the terminology and can drop the names 'file', 'record', 'field', and use instead: 'table', 'tuples' and 'attributes', which are the normal names when we are talking about databases. It is wrong to use these names interchangeably, but most people do and if you do, people will know what you are meaning so don't worry about them too much.

Databases are collections of data arranged into related tables. There are lots of ways of arranging the data in the tables and each arrangement can be given a label according to how it has been arranged. These labels are called their **Normal Form**. As far as we are concerned there are three types of normal form (although there are many more) and we are not very interested in the first two.

A database in first normal form (INF) is one where each table has no repeating groups. In our example, the attribute 'subjects studied' has been removed and a new table has been produced which has a separate record for each combination of student ID and subject. *In INF there are no attributes that have multiple data in them.*

A database in second normal form (2NF) is one where *the values of the attributes are all dependent on the primary key*. In our example the name of the student, the address, and other attributes relate specifically to the student so we can say that the StudentID determines name, address and emergency contact. However, just knowing the StudentID does not let us know who the student's teacher is, or which form room they are in and so these fields are not dependent on the StudentID. We need Subject to determine teacher, room and examlevel. We will also need a link between Student and subject – if we call it Takes then Takes determines StudentID and Subject. This is another reason for needing multiple tables.

A database in third normal form (3NF) 'has no attributes that are predictable because of one of the other attributes'. In our example, once we know what the form is we know the form teacher, so form teacher is dependent on form, not on StudentID, and for this reason it must be put in another table.

We end up with:

STUDENT(<u>StudentID</u>, Name, Address, Emergencycontact, Formname)

FORM(<u>Formname</u>, formteacher, formroom)

SUBJECT(<u>SubjectID</u>, Subject_name, teacher, room, examlevel)

TAKES(<u>StudentID</u>, <u>SubjectID</u>)

Do not worry too much about 1NF and 2NF, just their definitions, and the questions on 3NF tend to be fairly simple.

2. Methods and tools for analysing and implementing database design

Using the example of the student database that we are also developing, refer to the design of the tables above.

Each table contains one special attribute by which **tuples** can be identified because it is unique. As we saw in the previous section this is called the **primary key** and is shown by underlining its reference within the bracket of attributes. Note that two attributes are underlined in TAKES. StudentID cannot be the key because there will be a tuple for each subject that the student takes. SubjectID cannot be the key because there will be a tuple for every subject taken by a different pupil. The only solution is to combine the two attributes in a multiple (or composite) key.

A key in one table that occurs in another table is called a **foreign key**. It is used to link two tables together. In our example, if we wanted to find the form teacher for a particular student we would find the student using StudentID and then use Formname to go to the correct FORM to find the formteacher. In the full school database, formteacher may be a foreign key to a table of form teachers giving further details about each one.

A new type of key is called a **secondary key**. It is a field in a table that can be used to access the data in a different way. In the STUDENT table it may be sensible to store the tuples in alphabetical order according to the field Name, or according to Formname if the purpose is to print form lists.

< Discuss >

Discuss these results. Understand the way the tables are written down. Try to describe why they are in 3NF. Describe the way the tables are linked to each other.

It is possible to draw a diagram of the tables in a database.

The table names (known as Entities) go in boxes.

Figure 3.37

It doesn't matter what order the boxes are in although some orders will look tidier when we have finished.

Now we need to link the boxes.

Consider STUDENT and FORM. Every student is in one form and every form has lots of students in it. So, many students are in each form and this makes the link look like this:

Figure 3.38

This is a many-to-one relationship. (If the order of the boxes were the other way round it would be a one-to-many relationship, which is the same thing!)

What about STUDENT and SUBJECT? Every student takes many subjects and every subject is taken by many students, so, the diagram looks like this:

Figure 3.39

In 3NF we should never have a many-to-many relationship, so we have to put a new table/entity in the middle. This extra table is called a **link table** and is normally given a sensible name that demonstrates what it does. In our case we can call it TAKES.

Figure 3.40

This type of table is called a **link entity**. It normally consists of the key attributes of the tables on both sides and no additional data. Effectively, it is only there to get rid of the many-to-many relationship.

Our diagram now looks like this:

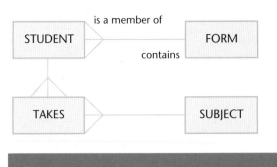

Figure 3.41

> **< Activity >**
>
> Notice the inclusion of the descriptors of the relationship between STUDENT and FORM. Provide the descriptors for the other relationships.

3. Database Management System (DBMS)

As we can see from our own, fairly simple example, a database can very quickly become complicated. It will need something to control it and to control access to it. It will need to control the amending of data to ensure that all the rules remain unbroken. The addition and deletion of data must also be controlled. The software (because that is all it is!) is called the **Database Management System**.

The DBMS includes a piece of software called **Data Description Language** (DDL).

The DDL is used to define the tables in the database; it also allows the designer to define data types and data structure within the database and any constraints on the data. The design that is created is called a **Schema**. Each user of the database will use it for different things, will be allowed to see different parts and will be given their own subschema to give the rules of how they see data.

Users of the database will be given different rights, but at least some will involve manipulating the data (e.g. to amend/delete/insert data). This is carried out using a tool called a **Data Manipulation Language** (DML).

The use of both the DDL and DML can be simplified with the provision by the DBMS of manipulation techniques like query by example (QBE).

The DBMS maintains a file of descriptions of the data and the structure of the storage of the data. This is known as the **data dictionary**.

The use of the various tools allows the DBMS to present various views of the data held within the database.

First there is the **internal level**. This is a view of the entire database as it is stored in the system. This is the level at which data is organised according to random access, indexed, sequential, etc. It is hidden from the user by the DBMS.

The second is the **conceptual level**, which gives a single, usable, view of all the data on the database.

< Discuss >

Using an expanded version of our example of a school admin database, discuss the different views that will be required by different people, or at different times, or at different terminals. Also consider how the different views at the external level can be 'policed'.

The third is the **external level**. This is where the data is arranged according to user requirements and rights. Different users will get different views of the data.

4. Use of Structured Query Language (SQL)

An **SQL** is a language that allows a user to set up their own queries on a database. It is nothing to worry about; the language uses the techniques and logical structures that were studied in Chapters 8 and 10.

All languages have a syntax and a number of command words. SQL is no different.

Generally, the syntax is to give a command word that tells the system what operation needs to be carried out and then instructions that tell the system the parts of the database on which this operation is to be done.

Consider the table FORM which we decided was to hold the attributes: Formname, Formteacher and Formroom. A section of the contents of the table might be:

Formname	Formteacher	Formroom
7AB	Mrs. Baker	31
7CG	Miss Greig	29
7DV	Ms Vincent	15
7JW	Ms Walker	22

Imagine that we want to delete 7CG from the table. What information would the system need? It would need to know that the intention was to delete (the command word). It would need to know the table to be used, in this case FORM. It would also need to know which record and how to identify it.

If you put all this information together and say it in English it would sound much like:

"Delete from FORM where Formname is 7CG." Translating into SQL syntax creates:

DELETE FROM Form WHERE Formname = '7CG'. The result would be:

Formname	Formteacher	Formroom
7AB	Mrs. Baker	31
7DV	Ms Vincent	15
7JW	Ms Walker	22

Some notes about this:

- Don't worry too much about the command words. There are more to come, but they will differ from one form of query language to another. As before, it is the logic that the examiner will be looking for.
- The content of the attribute is enclosed in quotes. This is very like data types when coding in a high-level language, for example, string or text variable values are enclosed in quotes while numeric values are not.
- Compare the SQL with the spoken English statement.

Imagine inserting a new row in the table:

"Insert into FORM the values 7BC, Mr Campbell, 21" translates as:

INSERT INTO Form VALUES ('7BC', 'Mr Campbell', 21). The result would be:

Formname	Formteacher	Formroom
7AB	Mrs. Baker	31
7DV	Ms Vincent	15
7JW	Ms Walker	22
7BC	Mr Campbell	21

Some more notes:

- Again, notice how close it is to English.
- The syntax of the statements may differ in your particular version of a lookup language, as it depends so much on the DBMS that is being used. The logic does not change.
- 21 did not need quotation marks because it is numeric.

The SELECT command word is very useful when creating reports because it allows specific pieces of information to be accessed from specific tables, for instance:

'Select all the data from FORM where Form teacher is Ms Walker'

SELECT * FROM Form WHERE Formteacher = 'Ms Walker'.

(Notice the use of * to stand for all the data). This will give:

7JW   Ms Walker   22

Imagine we wanted to find out where Ms Walker was. All we really need is the form room so we can narrow down the results by telling the system we want only the form room and not everything.

SELECT Formroom FROM Form WHERE Formteacher = 'Ms Walker'

This will give:
22

What will:

SELECT Formname FROM Form Where Formroom < 22

give?

It should give:
7DV   7BC

Explain why.

Notice that the full range of arithmetic operators can be used in the syntax.

< Activity >

Practice, in groups, producing some SQL, using our example table and also consider the STUDENT table.

Try to follow this SQL and describe what is happening.

SELECT name FROM STUDENT where Formname = 2G.

```
for    STUDENT
    if Formname = 2G then
                        print Name
        else
                        next Student ID
        end
end
```

4 The Project

1. Introduction

The project unit is a significant part of the A2 assessment and is worth 20% of the marks towards the A Level. Unlike the other units the student has some significant say in what this unit contains and can select a task that demonstrates their skills and ability. When selecting a project task the student should consider the syllabus requirements and how these can be demonstrated within the chosen task.

The moderators are looking for the application of knowledge and skills developed in the other three units to the solution of a realistic, real-world problem. The solution must contain a substantial coded element and the choice of problem and end user is crucial to success in this unit. While there are no restrictions on the choice of problem it is vital that the project provides sufficient opportunity to demonstrate the programming skills developed as part of the AS syllabus.

The choice of end user is an important consideration and the end user will need to be willing to comment on all stages of the design and development, including testing partial and complete solutions.

Figure 4.1 One-on-one interview

If the end user has a specific problem to be solved then a dialogue will need to be established and this dialogue recorded carefully as the project develops. If the end user simply identifies a potential problem then it may be appropriate to identify a focus group to help perform this role. For example, if the problem were to develop some educational software for use in a primary school, then, while the teacher remains the primary end user, a suitable focus group would include students in the target group who can comment on and trial the software as it is developed and once it is completed. If the problem were to develop a role playing game for 13–15-year-olds then a group of 13–15-year-olds would be a suitable supplementary focus group to the primary end user.

The student should not underestimate the amount of time required to complete this unit nor the amount of time the end user will have to give throughout the project. Ideally, work on this unit should start in the second half of the summer term after completing the AS modules.

This sort of long-term project needs to be carefully planned and it is best to break down the work into discrete smaller units with a series of deadlines throughout the year aimed at completion around the Easter holiday.

A good plan can make a significant difference to the progress and success of the project and should not be limited to an outline schedule typically represented in a Gantt chart.

Number	Task	Start	End	Duration	January	February	March	April	May	June
					2009					
1	Meet with end user to discuss project	05/01/2009	09/01/2009	5	■					
2	Analyse definitions and create investigation plan and interview questions	12/01/2009	27/01/2009	12	■					
3	Analyse data, collect documents and observe systems in action	28/01/2009	10/02/2009	10		■				
4	Develop requirements specification and agree with end user	11/02/2009	19/02/2009	7		■				
5	Create initial designs and discuss with end user	20/02/2009	27/02/2009	6		■				
6	Start prototyping the new system for end user	02/03/2009	13/03/2009	10			■			
7	Agreed designs developed and tested	16/03/2009	24/04/2009	30			■■			
8	Test finished system	27/04/2009	05/05/2009	7				■		
9	Write user documentation	06/05/2009	19/05/2009	10					■	

Figure 4.2

A good plan will include:

- an overview of what is to be achieved
- the system objectives and key requirements
- a description of how the project and individual sub problems will be tackled
- the outputs and key milestones in the development of the system
- the scope of the solution, that is, what is to be done and what is not included
- the resources required to complete the project, both hardware and software
- the key assumptions made in creating the project plan
- a schedule for carrying out the tasks, perhaps a Gantt chart or other representation of the time line to completion.

The student's role is that of systems analyst and a significant proportion of the marks are allocated to clear evidence of this. Interaction with the end user is vital and projects where the bulk of the information and feedback is from the students themselves are unlikely to score well in many sections.

30 of the 80 marks available for the project are awarded for development and testing, and while this is a significant proportion of the available marks, it is clear that the majority of the marks are awarded for the other processes. Providing the project chosen allows sufficient scope for the student to demonstrate the required skills – it would be unwise to select a problem that is too complex to complete comfortably within the time allocation.

The syllabus requires that the solution includes a substantial coded element but does not require a completely coded solution. While it is acceptable to take this route a more likely solution will contain sufficient coding to cover the syllabus requirements. This coded element can be completed in any suitable language and may be just a small part of the final solution. Whatever the balance between coded and application-generated elements it is vital the system meets the end user's needs.

2. Project selection

The project unit represents a significant proportion of the marks towards the A Level and takes a long time to complete. The selection of a suitable project can make a significant difference to the student's overall performance in this unit and consideration must be given to various factors.

The moderators use the marking criteria provided by OCR in appendix B of the syllabus as guidelines when assessing the work. Tutors and students should be familiar with these and students should select a project task that enables them to provide evidence that will meet these criteria. These criteria should not be regarded as pointing to any particular solution and many types of project will fit comfortably with these criteria.

The chosen project only has to meet the marking criteria and students should not over-stretch themselves with overly demanding projects. If the end user defines a problem that goes beyond the scope of the project then it might be possible for the student to target completion of just a small part of the proposed solution with the other work being identified as an extension to the developed system.

The end user will be required to give a significant amount of time at various stages of the development and the choice of end user should take this into consideration.

The syllabus imposes no restrictions on what applications or languages may be used and the student should aim to maximise their existing skills by using applications and languages with which they feel comfortable. There is a wide range of programming languages available to provide the student with opportunities to work in various areas, for example VBA to work with Access or Excel, Action scripts can demonstrate the required skills within Macromedia Flash projects, PHP within web-based projects, JAVA, Visual basic, C++, python, Ruby or any one of the many languages available for general programming use. OCR provide a coursework consultancy service and if in doubt about any proposed project idea or potential solution the tutor should contact them for advice.

Providing the chosen project meets the marking criteria the type of project is not restricted and data handling, financial control, web-based systems, control applications, educational games, computer utilities, graphics systems and many other possibilities can become realistic project tasks. BUT it is important to remember there are no extra marks for more complex problems and the student's choice should take this into account.

3. Investigation and analysis

Initially, very little may be known about the chosen problem area, but remember the moderator will have no information about the problem at all and the initial section in the report should set the scene. Identify the problem area, identify in broad terms what the task is and identify the end user(s). This brief introduction forms the basis for further investigation of the problem and a range of suitable systems analysis techniques should be used to identify what is required.

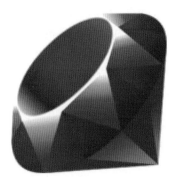

Figure 4.3 Some of the main programming languages

At this stage the student will have only superficial knowledge of the end user's requirements. Too much detail will imply that the problem is student-driven rather than end user-driven and this will limit the scope for interaction with the end user and consequently be self-penalising. The amount of detail expected is that which can be ascertained from a very brief preliminary interview or from brief contact with the potential end user.

This section of the report should include:

- who the end user is and what they or their organisation do/does
- what role the end user plays in their organisation
- what problem the end user has identified as needing a solution for in general terms
- what sort of data or information might be involved.

There should be some evidence to support how these assertions have been identified. This initial contact forms the basis for the next stage and how the student intends to investigate the proposed problem.

4. Investigating the problem

After the initial contact with the end user, and with a basic idea of what the end user requires, the student should formulate a plan to ascertain detailed requirements from the end user. This will involve an interview with the end user, which should be carefully planned, with a set of primary and subsidiary questions to ensure the interview provides sufficient detail to prepare for the next stage in the process. The interview will normally be carried out face-to-face but it is equally valid to carry out the interview stage by telephone, email or even by letter. Whichever method or range of methods are used it is important that original notes are presented in the report to the moderator. Remember to build sufficient flexibility into the planning in order to follow up any unexpected issues that may arise during the interview. It is also advisable to inform the end user about the process in advance and to identify what information they will need to have to hand during the interview. It may also be appropriate to contact more than one person within the organisation in order to ascertain the requirements.

Figure 4.4 Student interviewing an end user

If there is an existing system in place then there may be a range of documents and reports to collect. It should be possible to observe and/or discuss current practices, data flows and any other issues. Notes should be kept and used in the report to the moderator.

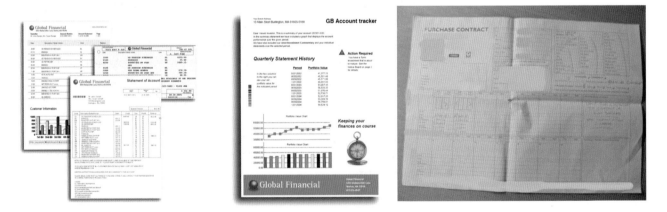

Figure 4.5 Documentation from end user

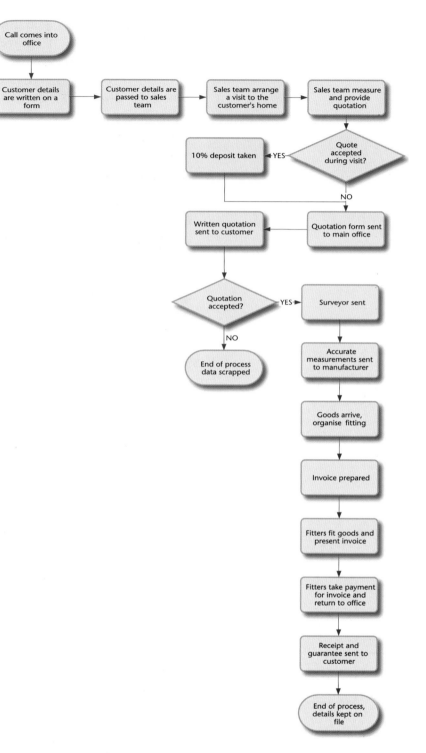

Figure 4.6

For a new system discussions with the end user and contact with any focus group should identify their requirements. Investigation of similar systems may also help inform what is possible and what is required.

This is a vital stage in the process that will determine the course of the project. At the first meeting with the end user(s) an outline of what the system should do has been identified. The following process should establish a detailed specification that could be passed on to another developer to complete.

Dialogue between the end user and the analyst needs to establish detailed criteria, and interviews, whether face-to-face or via email or otherwise, should be carefully planned, with suitable supplementary questions based on the responses from the end user. Establishing sufficient detail is unlikely to come from a single meeting and supplementary questioning to clarify aspects of the final requirements should take place. Questionnaires can also provide useful feedback on proposals, especially if the end user is asking for a system others are likely to use.

If there is an existing system to replace or develop then there may well be input and output documents, user guides, screen designs and other items that can be collected to inform the analysis of the problem. Observation of the current system in action will also provide considerable insight into how the current system performs, its inadequacies and how the new system might be developed.

Figure 4.7 Observation in the workplace

If there is no existing system more reliance has to be put on discussions with the end user and it is appropriate to produce outline prototypes, screen designs, and other suggestions to take back to the end user for discussion. There may also be similar systems available to investigate and inform judgements.

In both cases it is important to establish what data is likely to be used and how. For existing systems typical data can be identified and data flows within the system established or, with new systems, the end user(s) should consider what data is likely and how this data might flow through the system.

This section of the report should include:

- detailed interview planning including who is being interviewed, when, where, why and how
- a record of the interview stages including:
  - the original interview questions and any subsidiary questions used
  - original notes from the interview, for example any notes taken, original emails with headers, letters, notes and transcripts of telephone conversations
- any original documents and sample data from an existing system
- notes from observations or discussions with other potential users
- evidence of further research, for example research into existing similar systems
- possibly, data flow diagrams, system flow charts or similar methods to show how the current system works.

5. Analysing the data collected

Figure 4.8 Agreement on a deal

The data and opinions collected during this stage should be recorded and analysed to produce a requirements specification to present to the end user for their approval. This will generally be a cyclic process and the final end user requirements will be arrived at after a series of discussions and refinements. This requirements specification will form the basis of the contract between the end user(s) and the developer against which success or failure will be evaluated. Keep it straightforward and identify a brief, sensible and achievable set of criteria.

Figure 4.9 A suitable printer should be specified

The information collected during the investigation phase should be analysed to pick out the key issues. It is important to use the results of the investigation to justify that these are the key points and that the end user(s) have been consulted. This section of the project is essentially a report back to the end user(s) explaining how you have interpreted their responses and other information collected to create a specification that meets their requirements.

Any requirements specification must also identify the hardware and software requirements for the final system. These hardware and software requirements must also be justified in terms of what the system should achieve and must be related back to the data collected during the investigation stage. For example, if the specification includes printing a report, then a suitable printer should be specified. Hardware and software specifications should be specific and include minimum and recommended requirements. It is not sufficient to specify what system the end user has and simply say it is 'more than adequate'; the end user(s) may wish to use the system elsewhere.

Figure 4.9 A suitable printer should be specified

Recommended system requirements
PC (Client/Standalone) Windows 2000 (SP4), XP SP2 (Home & Pro), Vista
PC (Server) Windows 2000 and 2003
Mac (Client/Standalone) Mac OS X 10.3 or higher; G4, G5 or Intel processor
Mac (Server) G5 or higher

1GB hard disc space is required to install the title. The minimum screen resolution is 1024 x 768. A sound card is also required. A fast processor (PC, 1GHz; Mac, 1.25 GHz) and good graphics card is recommended. Server requirements are higher.
Some files on this DVD-ROM require the use of Microsoft Word, PowerPoint, Publisher, Excel and Access as well as access to the Internet.

Figure 4.10 Recommended system requirements for a piece of educational software

This section of the report should include:

- a detailed and justified requirements specification agreed with the end user. (Make sure the end user signs off this section)
- justified hardware and software requirements for the proposed solution.

Analysing the data collected

6. Design

Figure 4.11 Designer

The choice of task will dictate much of the content for this section but the student must bear in mind the syllabus requirements and ensure each item in the marking criteria is covered in sufficient detail.

The end user has agreed to a set of requirements for the proposed solution and these should be turned into a specific set of system objectives. The student needs to take each of the requirements and decide what needs to be done by the time the project is completed. These objectives must be objective, rather than subjective – in other words, a list of measurable criteria that can obviously be proven to have been achieved or not.

For example:

"Mr Smith needs to be able to input details of individual sales."

"The system should produce a report showing total sales for the month grouped by sales person."

It is easy to provide evidence that objectives like those listed above have been achieved, but objectives like "The screen layout is pleasant to look at" or "The system is easy to use" require judgment as to their success or not. Subjective objectives are not easily proven and should be avoided.

The objectives will form the basis for the design and development of the system and should be related back to the requirements specification to show how they were derived. They will also form the basis for the final testing and the evaluation stages and should be agreed with the end user. Since it is a requirement for the end user to agree to and sign off these objectives, it is not unreasonable for the final set of objectives to be changed by agreement between the student and the end user at this stage, or even later in the development process. Agreeing to a final set of objectives is not likely to be achieved in a single meeting and the student will need to provide evidence of how these objectives have developed in consultation with the end user during the development of the system. Rather than seeing significant changes as evidence of difficulties the student should realise that negotiating a final set of objectives is a normal part of the process and provides excellent evidence for end user involvement.

Figure 4.12

These system objectives help the developer to produce detailed system designs. At the end of this stage the designs should be detailed enough to pass on to another developer to create an identical system.

Designs for all input documents, data collection forms and input screens should be created and agreed with the end user, as should designs for output reports, screens and other forms of output, for example, audio. A mock-up of the user interface also needs to be created and agreed with the end user before any development begins. It is reasonable and likely that these designs will be adjusted during the development process but initial ideas need to be established and agreed before the work commences.

Data used within the system will need to be stored and accessed accurately and efficiently. The data flows within the system need to be identified, as do the data structures to hold the data, and this section should also include outline designs for all record, file and data structures required. For example, all arrays and data files with an indication of what they will contain and data validation needs to be identified at this stage.

Describing processes, data flows and structures may be easier using a diagram and it is important to remember that the moderator is looking for clarity rather than correct use of data flow diagrams or system flowcharts. A combination of simple diagrams, written descriptions, simple flowcharts which convey clearly how the system will function is more than adequate, though if the student wishes to use one of the many systems available to represent data flows or systems, then by all means, go ahead.

This section of the report should include:

■ a list of specific measurable objectives for the system, which should be agreed with and signed off by the end user
■ any necessary data collection which needs to be identified and described
■ detailed descriptions of how data is to be input into the system, including screen designs
■ detailed descriptions of data output including screen and/or printed report designs and details of any other outputs from the system
■ data structures, file structures, data types and validation to be used
■ an explanation of how data is manipulated by the system
■ a description of how the system works in diagrammatic or other form, including input to and output from the system.

7. Rules, methods, algorithms and test strategies

The syllabus requires a substantial part of the project solution to be coded using a suitable high-level modular language. This section deals largely with that part of the project that is to be coded but needs to be related to the overall solution if it is to convey in sufficient detail how the system fits together.

Once the design is completed it will be possible to prepare detailed process models using suitable techniques including top-down analysis, algorithms and pseudo-code. These process models need to be tested to ensure they perform as required and meet the design objectives.

Algorithms can be presented in many forms, including flowcharts, pseudo-code and top-down designs, but essentially they are detailed sets of instructions showing in order what tasks are performed and how they are interrelated. The moderator will be looking for clear explanations of how the components of the system function and how they fit together. The moderator will also expect to see clear evidence of how each component has been tested to show that it produces the desired output and that the components function together to achieve the desired result.

Testing these algorithms might be completed using dry runs with typical test data or any other suitable method, but careful planning is essential and should be related to specific system objectives from the design section.

This section of the report should include:

- an overview of how the system components fit together
- a complete set of algorithms for the system
- evidence of testing to show that the individual algorithms perform as required
- evidence to show that the components fit together to produce the desired outcomes.

8. Test strategy

A significant proportion of the testing will need to be completed during the development stages if the student is to ensure that the system achieves the design objectives. It is important to plan the test strategy before the system is developed rather than rely on post development testing which concentrates on what the system can do rather than what it should do. The test strategy and suitable test data should be agreed with the end user in order to test the system thoroughly throughout the development of the solution.

Test data needs to be selected for each element of the test strategy to ensure all possibilities are covered: typical values, extreme valid and invalid data on and just outside designed limits and invalid data values and types. For example, if a variable can take integer values between 1 and 5 inclusive then suitable data would include:

Valid data 2

Invalid data -1, apple, 2.12, 15

Extreme valid data 1, 5

Extreme invalid data 0, 6

This data will be the data used during development to test individual segments of the solution and at the end of the process to test the overall function of the system. Test data needs to be identified to cover as many eventualities as possible but as a minimum should cover all aspects of the requirements specification and design objectives. The test strategy should identify what is being tested, what data is being used and what is the expected result.

This section of the report should include:

- an overall description of the test strategy
- test data covering normal, abnormal and extreme conditions, together with the expected results for that data.

9. Software development and testing

It is up to the student to show how the system has been developed and tested. This section should include evidence of how the solution relates to the design specification and of how each of the elements has been developed, tested and modified if necessary during the development phase. All the work in this section needs to be clearly annotated to show the process, including testing, which identifies the need for changes in the system. There should be clear evidence of the designed data structures being implemented and evidence of input and output to the system. Data files should be shown to work with printouts of the data before and after changes as well as functional testing of the components in the system. Finally, the completed system should be tested, including clear evidence that the end user has been involved in the process.

The coded elements of the system must be fully annotated and there should be evidence that these have been thoroughly tested during development. 'Fully annotated' means, that if the code were removed, the annotation would be sufficient to rewrite the code precisely.

Figure 4.13 Advising on use of the new software

It is important to remember that the moderator may not be familiar with the programming language and/or any other software packages being used, but will be able to understand the relevant logical processes. The evidence in this section of the report should take this into account and evidence should concentrate on clarifying the processes and logic of the development process.

Remember that any work credited must be the work of the candidate and if code or other elements are taken from other sources without significant modification then this must be credited to the appropriate source.

This section of the report should include:

- annotated evidence of development
- evidence of input and output screens and reports as appropriate
- evidence of data structures
- evidence of files before and after changes are made
- evidence of white box testing during implementation and any changes that are made as a result of this testing
- fully annotated code.

10. Testing the system

The final solution must be tested to ensure it achieves the stated design objectives. Full testing will include the white box testing completed as part of the development, alpha testing completed by the student on the final system and beta testing completed by the end user on the system. Remember it is unlikely the student will be able to test every aspect of the system and as a minimum each aspect of the solution mentioned in the requirements specification should be included.

The system should be tested using the data from the test strategy in the design section and should include typical data, extreme data and invalid data and data types. Functional testing should also be included to show that basic navigation through the system is effective and accurate.

Evidence of actual results using the test data from the design test strategy should be related to the strategy to indicate success or otherwise and any modifications as a result of testing should be identified, implemented and re-tested as necessary.

The report for this section should include:

- evidence of developer testing using the design test strategy with appropriate comments on success or otherwise and this should be related to the original strategy
- evidence of any modifications completed as a result of testing
- evidence of end user testing with typical data.

11. User documentation

The system should include good onscreen documentation to help the end user make efficient use of the system and marks in this section depend upon the quality and detail of this onscreen documentation rather than on a paper-based user guide. However, there should be some necessary, supplementary documentation to cover installation, basic troubleshooting, system requirements and getting started to ensure the end user can implement the system. The overall documentation package should provide a detailed and comprehensive guide to the system in a clear, easy-to-follow and user-friendly format.

A significant proportion of the marks for this section will be awarded for the user documentation included within the solution rather than for a bulky printed user guide. Good onscreen help is essential and the final solution should include clear informative screen layouts, informative error messages, context-sensitive help and online help files where appropriate. The student should provide evidence for this online user support by producing a suitable set of printouts, possibly by reference to the main test evidence in the previous section.

Some printed user documentation is still essential to complete this section and should include those printed items normally found with a new piece of software. For example:

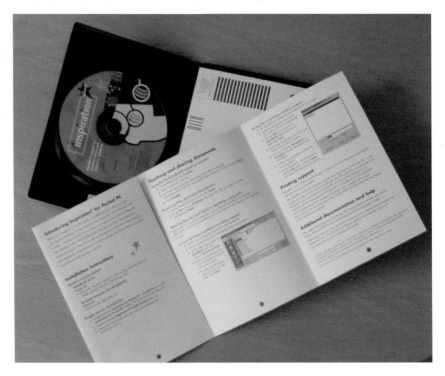

Figure 4.14 Supplementary documentation

Getting started: to help the user install and set up the system, including hardware and software requirements and how to install and start using the system.

Troubleshooting: explaining how to deal with typical problems not relating to normal usage and not covered by the built-in error messages.

Security: explaining how to secure the data and suggested backup routines.

This section of the report should include:

- evidence of onscreen support, including error messages and any online help files
- supporting printed documentation, including 'getting started', 'troubleshooting' and 'security'.

12. Evaluation

The final system should be evaluated against the original requirements. Taking each of the items specified in the original specification and the evidence produced during the testing phases it should be possible to indicate how well the final product matches the original requirements. It is possible that changes were made to the original specification as the project developed and these should also be documented with comments on why the changes were made and indicating any evidence available to show how the revised specification was achieved. Test evidence from the end user should also be used to show how the final solution compares to the one agreed at the start of the process.

This section of the report should include:

- a point by point discussion of the original agreed objectives taken from the requirements specification, with reference to the evidence in the rest of the report, to show how these were met or to explain why they were not met.
- references to testing completed by the end user, discussing how well the system matches the end user's expectations of the system.

13. Evaluation of the users' responses

During the development the end user will have been involved with decisions and testing. The developer should discuss with the end user(s) any comments made by the end user(s) and the results from end user testing to indicate how any criticisms or inadequacies were or could be dealt with.

When developing a system for an end user we cannot expect the end user to be comfortable with any subject-specific jargon, or to be comfortable with a basic interface. Systems produced for end users need to be made user-friendly and to include good onscreen instructions and help. All of these items will contribute to the overall end user satisfaction with the system and should be commented upon by the developer in this section.

Figure 4.15 The project is finished

The end user should also provide feedback based on their experience with the system, commenting on the system in general terms, the things they could do, the things they could not do and any improvements that need to be made to make the system match their original expectations.

This section of the report should include:

- written feedback from the end user following testing commenting on how well the system matches their expectations and any improvements that might be required
- comments from the student on the feedback from the end user.

14. Evaluation of the final system

Having completed the process it is time to reflect on the whole process and comment on the overall success of the project. Good and not so good aspects of the system should be identified and comments made on any limitations in the system. It is also likely that the system could be developed further and the developer should comment on any improvements or developments that could be made and should also indicate how these might be achieved.

However well the system has performed there will be things that can be improved, especially given the limited time available to the student to take on a real world task for this module. It is important that the student shows that they are aware of this and discusses how they would take the project forward from this stage. All sorts of issues can be discussed, including hardware availability, software choices, end user imposed limitations, modifications to designs, sections not completed because of time restrictions, etc. The student should also be prepared to say what they have done well and show that they are aware of particularly good aspects of the system they have developed or the bits that show how clever they have been.

This section of the report should include:

- a list of satisfactorily completed elements in the solution
- a list of those elements that are not satisfactory, the reason why the student thinks this and what they might have done about this if time was available to do so
- a list of areas not included that would improve the solution and how these might have been approached
- comments on the best aspects of the system.

15. The project report

The project report should be largely written as a report on the process for the moderator. The one exception to this is the requirements specification, which should be written as a report back to the end user on the analysis of their requirements and justifying the proposed system.

The report should be clearly presented with page numbers, an index and clearly identified sections. The moderator will not be able to spend hours searching through the report and the student stands to lose marks if evidence is not clearly identified in the report and cannot be easily located.

The report should be presented in the same order as the marking criteria in appendix B of the OCR syllabus, with ALL evidence to support a section included within the appropriate part of the report. While it is common practice to supply evidence in real world systems analysis in appendices, these reports are aimed not at the end user, to whom this evidence may be peripheral, but at the moderator and, as such, are not typical systems analysis reports. For example, interview notes and evidence collected during the analysis and investigation phase should be included within that section as supplementary pages interleaved with the main body of the report. Test evidence should be included at the appropriate point in the report, as should evidence from the end user testing and end user feedback.

Since much of the testing takes place during development and the evidence belongs within that section the testing section can quite legitimately refer to test evidence in other sections without penalty, as can evidence used to support the evaluation of the project.